Real Estate Investments: What you need to Know

By Edward S. Smith, Jr.
CREI, ITI, CIC, GREEN, MICP, CNS
CIREC Program Developer

Second Edition: Updated and revised to reflect the new 2018 tax laws.

My goal with this book is to help new and experienced investors to understand the simplicity and complexity of investing in real estate. It will define the terms, concepts and formulas you should know, and will examine the benefits and potential problems of real estate investments. A number of years ago I wrote another book on investing, but since the real estate industry is constantly changing a new updated and expanded look at real estate investing is needed.

In this book we will look at market history, investment basics, financial analysis, financing today, owning property, being a landlord, selling your property and other things you need to know. We will specifically examine recent changes in the market, new laws, tax changes (the good and the bad), green buildings, leasing and much more will be explored.

Edward S. Smith, Jr.

Other books by the author:

Understand Green: Concerns, Concepts and Practices – Amazon

Formulas and Calculations: Using the HP10BII+ Calculator – Amazon

The Commercial Classroom Volume 2 - Amazon

Commercial and Investment Real Estate: Tools of the Trade – Dearborn Publishing

Commercial Real Estate: Listing Properties – Dearborn Publishing

Commercial Real Estate: Understanding Investments – Dearborn Publishing

Commercial Real Estate: Smart Marketing Practices – Dearborn Publishing

The Commercial Classroom – Amazon

Buy the Numbers: Investing in Real Estate – Amazon

About the Author

Edward S. Smith, Jr., is currently a Real Estate Instructor and Consultant. He is a licensed Real Estate Broker in Connecticut and New York, specializing in Commercial and Investment Real Estate, with over 40 years of brokerage experience. For eleven years, prior to 2015, he was Regional Director for Coldwell Banker Commercial NRT in CT and NY. He previously served as a "Consultant to the Trade" and had his own Brokerage firm.

He has authored nine other books on commercial real estate, including four textbooks with instructor training materials used to teach commercial courses throughout the United States. He has written a monthly column "The Commercial Classroom", for the New York Real Estate Journal for the past fifteen years and has over 180 published articles on Commercial and Investment Real Estate.

Mr. Smith is an Instructors Training Institute (ITI) graduate and has 19 years' experience teaching real estate courses. He has developed over a dozen continuing education courses and the Commercial and Investment Real Estate Certification Programs.

Currently, he serves on the Boards of Directors of the New York City-Long Island Chapter of NYSCAR, and the Long Island Commercial Network (LICN).

He is Past President of: the New York State Commercial Association of Realtors® (NYSCAR), the Metro-LI Chapter of NYSCAR and the Long Island Commercial Network. He has also served as a Director of the New York State Association of Realtors, the Long Island Board of Realtors® and the Real Estate Practitioners Institute at Long Island University. He is a former Officer and Director of the Commercial Industrial Brokers Society (CIBS).

Visit the Authors web site at: www.CommercialEd.com

Edward S. Smith, Jr.

Table of Contents

Preface

This is a great time to invest in real estate.

Buying a home gives consideration to many things, layout, number of bedrooms, baths, the kitchen, yard and of course price. Other factors are also very important: location, schools, the neighborhood, community resources, proximity to hospitals and mass transportation. Finding a building to house your business is also largely based upon location, location, location. Where will be business be most successful? Purchasing these properties are also investments; by anticipating a future growth in value. But the main focus is living or working there.

More traditional investments will be properties that you totally rent to others or a business property you occupy that is larger than your needs, and the surplus space is rented out. In these cases you need to buy, based the numbers (the financials). What will be the return on your investment now, next year, the year after that, and when you sell it? How do you evaluate a potential purchase? How do you do a financial analysis and value projections? What type of building should you invest in? Can you get financing? What do you need to know about the Americans with Disability Act? Should you improve the building, make it "green"? What about leasing, income taxes, capital gains taxes? These questions and many others will be answered in this book.

When purchasing investment properties we need to consider location but timing is also critically important. Timing is everything and this is the right time. All investments have a level of risk, especially if you buy speculatively on the short term. But investing in real estate for the longer term has been a proven winner. People who bought real estate 15 – 20 years ago saw their investments grow substantially in value, sure there are periodic downturns in markets and some value may be temporarily lost. But look at the big picture, what is the property worth today verses what was paid for it.

With investment property you don't have to wait until you sell it to make a profit. Investment properties produce cash flows, giving you an annual return on your investment. In recent year's property values declined, they are now stabilized and starting to rise, plus leasing rates are increasing again too. Timing to make your investments is important and now is the right time.

It is hoped this book will give a clear understanding of investment terms, concepts and facts to help one buy wisely and protect your real estate investments. Real estate is still the best investment!

Part 1

Market History

Chapter 1: The "Perfect Storm"

A **"perfect storm"** is an expression that describes an event where a rare combination of circumstances will aggravate a situation drastically. [Wikipedia]

The 'perfect storm" hit the real estate industry in 2007-2008, due to a combination of the end of a real estate cycle, "criminal" underwriting of loans, the unscrupulous packaging and sale of those loans and other economic events.

Real estate values go through cycles. Visualize a roller coaster rising slowly, reaching a peak and then coming down again usually at greater speed. Periodically, values climb so high, that the markets can no longer function and adjustments are necessary. In these cycles property values slowly rise for many years; the market reaches a peak and then over a few years drops dramatically. The cycle may take ten years or in the case of the latest rise and fall even longer. But history has shown these real estate patterns will continue.

Fortunately, by 2013 in most areas, commercial markets had stabilized. We have come out of the latest depressed market, values have been adjusted and real estate is again starting to appreciate. We are now in the next cycle and values will increase again, slowly but steadily. This is actually a great time to invest in real estate.

It is important to understand that the last "real estate cycle" was not the only contributing factor to the loss of property values we experienced from 2008 to 2012. As we reached the peak of the cycle interest rates were extremely low and bad underwriting of loans fueled the oncoming crash. Mortgage underwriting in the early and mid- 2000's became "loose", no money down loans, no income checks, adjustable mortgages, low interest rates, "don't worry about tomorrow" thinking. Fog a mirror and you get a loan!

The processing and approving of loans for unqualified applicants became ramped and in some cases was criminal. By 2007, the effects were starting to be seen, people could not make their mortgage payments, loans were being defaulted on. This "mortgage meltdown" was one of the major causes of the real estate market to crash in 2007-2008.

The financial crash was further fueled by the creation of Mortgage Backed Securities (MBS) which included these risky "subprime" mortgages. [A Mortgage Backed Security is an asset-based security, secured by a group of mortgages. Typically an Investment Bank or government entity like Fannie Mae or Freddie Mac buys mortgages and packages groups of them together as MBS, and then sell them to investors.]

By 2007 almost all MBS's being sold contained mostly sound and paid on time mortgages, but also were bundled with "high risk" loans. At that time $100's of Billions of these MBS were sold to banks, pension funds and investors. The sale of these "toxic" real estate assets, mostly Fanny Mae backed mortgages, caused the "Liquity Crisis" in September, 2007.

In 2008 the government took control of Fannie Mae and Freddie Mac, who had lost over $15 Billion dollars, and caused worldwide consequences to investors and created millions of foreclosures.

In October of 2008 the Emergency Economic Stabilization Act of 2008 was passes in response to the "Subprime Crisis". It authorized the Secretary of the Treasury to spend $700 Billion to purchase distressed assets, especially Mortgage Backed Securities and supply cash directly to banks. This action bailed out and saved many banks from failure.

Another consequence of the crisis was the stock market, it actually peaked on October 9, 2007, but by mid 2008 had lost 20% in value. On September 29, 2008 the market

Had another huge loss dropping 778 points, and it continued to decline. Finally it bottomed out on March 6, 2009 with overall losses in stock values from 30% to 54%. Many people lost tremendous amounts of their retirement and 401 accounts. The market subsequently rebounded but was in turbulence again in 2016.

The casualties of the combined crisis's included: Washington Mutual Bank (6th largest in U.S.) and 417 other banks closed by federal regulators, Lehman Brothers Bankrupted, AIG Insurance Company only saved by an $85 Billion U.S. bailout. Merrill Lynch, at that time, valued its Mortgage Backed Security holdings at $.22 cents on the dollar. The company was only saved from bankruptcy by a Bank of America takeover. Many other companies and investors suffered and worst of all, there were over 20 Million residential foreclosures between 2007 - 2013.

The Dodd Frank Bank Reform Bill in July, 2010 put forth new regulations to prevent this sort of economic disaster from ever occurring again. As part of the Dodd Frank Committee investigation, as to the cause of the financial crisis, 900,000 mortgages issued between 2006 - 2008 were reviewed. 46% of these loans did not meet the originators underwriting standards. Of these 39% were securitized and sold to investors.

Two major steps were taken the creation of a Consumer Financial Protection Agency to "watchdog" banks, that they do not lend without borrowers being employed, having legitimate income and good credit; aimed specifically at preventing no document home loans. Second, Mortgage Backed Securities and now being regulated by the Commodity Futures Trading Commission and must be insured against default.

The down side of the latest real estate cycle lasted until 2013. It is unfortunate that many homeowners and investors were hurt when the values declined. But most of the economic problems really were a result of unscrupulous lending and security practices.

By 2016 the economy had strengthened, there are new underwriting standards both for residential and commercial loans, the unscrupulous mortgage companies were out of business, mortgage backed securities are regulated and real estate activity is strong.

Now in 2018, the commercial and investment real estate market is robust, with values in most markets back to pre-2007 levels or higher.

Part 2
Investment Basics

Chapter 2: Common Investment Terms

Invest 1: to commit (money) in order to earn a financial return **2:** to expend for future benefits or advantages **3:** to make an investment

Investment: the outlay of money for income or profit: *also*: the sum invested or the property purchased

(Definitions quoted from The Merriam Webster Dictionary)

The profit on a cash investment is usually referred to as the **return on investment (ROI).**

A return on an investment may also be in the form of an **appreciation** in the value of the investment where the value of the item (investment) today exceeds the price that was originally paid for it. A painting is bought for $100 and ten years later it is sold for $250 - it appreciated in value $150. Your home purchased ten years ago would generally be worth more today than what you paid for it. The gain in value is the appreciation.

Returns on investments may also be in the form of **cash flows,** funds that are received periodically during the term (ownership) of the investment. Depositing money into a bank savings account will result in the bank paying interest on the account. Each month the earned interest is added to the account balance. This represents a positive cash flow and if not withdrawn a periodic increase in the value of the investment. In real estate the resulting cash flow, after reconciling the income and expenses of a property is referred to as the **Net Operating Income (NOI).**

Some investments offer the opportunity for both appreciation and cash flows. An investment in stocks or bonds may produce a growth in the value over time (appreciation) and also produce dividends (cash flows). Investment properties generally produce annual cash flows and appreciate over time.

Not all investments, however, always perform favorably. In some cases losses of value or negative cash flows may occur. Great care must be taken when investing. Consideration must be given to the **risk** involved and the **level of owner management** required. Risk usually relates to the level of potential return (profit) on the investment. Placing one's money in a bank savings account would be considered low risk but the return (interest rate) would also be relatively low. There also would be little concern for management of the account by the investor.

A stock investment may yield a higher return, but there is also risk that the stock value may go down and could even create a loss of principal (the initial investment amount). More attention (time) of the owner is required to manage this type of investment.

Investing in real estate will have varying levels of risk and management. Buying your own home is an investment in real estate. It is hoped that when the day comes to sell it the house will have appreciated in value. Generally this would be considered a low risk investment and not require any management. Buying an investment property with three tenants may produce a positive cash flow and an opportunity for appreciation. But, what happens if one of the tenants leaves; how long will it take to find a replacement tenant? How would this affect the "bottom line"? Here elements of risk do come into consideration. If the property needs substantial repair in the future could this cause a negative cash flow in that year? Consideration must also be given to how much time will be required to manage the property. Sometimes hiring a building manager or management company alleviates this.

Another concern of many investors is **liquidity**, how fast can the investment be turned back into cash. A bank account investment, where the money can be almost immediately withdrawn would represent high liquidity. A painting or art as an investment may take quite a while to sell and would be considered low liquidity. Real estate because it can take some time to sell a property and even more time to actually close the sale is considered to have low liquidity.

Certain investments may be **leveraged** whereby the investor puts up an **initial investment,** a portion of the purchase price, and another entity finances the balance of the cost. The most common example would be in real estate where a mortgage is obtained, typically from a bank, the buyer's initial investment being the down payment and the loan being repaid over a number of years. The amount of principal and interest repaid to the bank each year is known as the **annual debt service.** When property is leveraged the return on the investment is known as the **Cash on Cash Return.**

Another example of this concept is available in the purchase of stocks and is known as buying on **margin**. Here money is borrowed from the stockbroker to buy a stock and the stock is used as the collateral for the loan. This increases the purchasing power of the investor so they can own more stock without fully paying for it. However, a margin purchase may also expose the investor to potential for higher losses if the value of the stock decreases.

Taxation of income occurs annually when the investment produces interest, dividends, or positive cash flows; losses may produce tax adjustments. The appreciation gained on an investment at the time of sale will also be subject to taxation. Taxation methods vary according to the type of investment. All tax related matters should be discussed with an accountant or a tax advisor.

With real estate there will be property taxes due each year. There may be income taxes due as a result of positive cash flows and **capital gains taxes** may be required when the property is sold. (This will be discussed in a later chapter.)

Yield (Rate of Return) – An indication of how the investment is doing, expressed in percentage terms based on the rate of return for each dollar invested. This is measured as either before or after tax dollars.

Chapter 3: Types of Investments

Your home as an investment

The "American Dream" is to own your own home. What varies immensely is what it takes to do so. Which jobs are available and what typical wages are, is generally reflected in the cost of houses in that specific area. Most regions will have a range of style and values, but that range will be based on the local economy. Purchasing your own home will require a down payment and the ability to obtain mortgage financing. The bank or lending institution will look at the borrowers "cash flow" (income and other expenses) to determine if it is sufficient to pay back the loan. Mortgage programs, the required down payment percentages, income requirements and interest rates all reflect local economic conditions.

In selecting a home most people base it upon the size and needs of their family and obviously what they can afford. There are choices in style; do you want to buy a condominium, a co-op, a single family house, a duplex or a multi-family? Which will be the best long term investment? In making this decision beside the comfort and convenience of where you will live, consider that for many this is the biggest investment of their lives. For most people there will come a point when the property will be sold. What is the appreciation potential of this investment?

Buying a duplex (two family houses) or a multi-family to live in adds the value of income to your investment. Income(s) from your tenant(s) which will help you pay the building's expenses and mortgage loan. This also gives you another option when you decide to sell your property. The building could be sold to another person like you who wished to live in the building and have income deferring costs, or it may be purchased by a pure investor who would rent out all the units.

Types of Commercial Investment Properties

Basically any building can be an investment. All that is needed is a tenant paying rent. There are five primary classifications of commercial properties: office, retail, industrial, apartments and land. Land may be held for future development or land may be leased.

Office Buildings are classified as Class A, Class B, Class C or Medical.

The Class A building is considered to be the "best available space" and is the most expensive. These buildings are generally newer and feature superior architecture, often with massive atriums. They are located near major roadways, with easy access and have excessive available parking. Many have amenities for the building tenants, like health clubs, child care facilities and upscale restaurants in addition to cafeterias. Pricing Class A properties "pushes" the market, consistently getting the highest rent possible. Tenants in these building are often Fortune 500 companies or major corporations. Why do these firms pay this exorbitant rent? They are buying "image", they are making a statement to their customers. We can afford to be in this building because we are the best at what we do, so you should become our customer.

I like to think of Class B buildings as a "tired Class A". At one time these buildings were the best available, but perhaps 10 or 15 years have passed and now someone has constructed a new more modern building in the area – a new Class A. Effectively this lowers the rating of these former Class A buildings to Class B. These are still good buildings, there is just a better newer building available. Regional firms such as large law firms or corporate headquarter type of tenants often occupy this type of property. The rent in the Class B building is usually 10% to 20% less than what the Class A building charge. It is also possible that a developer will intentionally build a Class B office building.

Class C office buildings take two forms, they can be an older building, maybe 40, 50 or 60 years old or they can be purposely built. The older building may have a beautiful marble foyer and staircase but no elevator! In the summer air conditioning units dangle from the windows as there is no central air conditioning. These properties are considered to be reaching "structural obsolescence". A builder today can construct a Class C building; it will be plain, simple box construction, just to comply with the building code. This type of building is generally found in the downtown areas. Tenants in these buildings are not concerned with "image". Most do not have their customers coming to their location. Typical tenants might include a bank back office operation, a telemarketing company or a sales office where all the salespersons are in the field. Pricing Class C space is geographic in nature. It is based on the local economics of the property's location.

Medical space is different from other office buildings. Visualize a typical doctor's office. It consists of many small examining rooms all of which have a sink in them. The cost of building a medical office is higher due to the extensive plumbing requirements and other construction issues. Consequently when a building is constructed for medical use, it usually stays that way. The construction costs more so the value and rent is higher. The rent is also based upon the economics at the buildings location.

Retail Properties can range from a small store on Main Street to our mega-malls. Free Standing Buildings as the name implies are not attached to any other structure. On the smaller side these are typically fast food restaurants, banks, coffee stores and they often have drive-through windows. Larger buildings such as drug stores, supermarkets, department stores and home improvement stores are also often free standing.

The next category is "strip centers". These structures are generally rectangular buildings housing 6 to 10 stores. The construction typically allows for the walls separating stores to be removed or added thus creating flexibility in the store sizes. The stores on each end of the strip center are known as "End Caps", which may provide signage on two sides of possible drive-through use. The interior stores are called "In Line". The "End Caps" rent for more money.

When we start combining our larger stores with our smaller stores we create a shopping center. When this occurs the largest store, which may be a supermarket or department store, would be referred to as the "Anchor Store". Anchor stores do extensive advertising thus bringing customers to both their store and the surrounding small stores in the shopping center. A landlord will typically discount the rent to get a good Anchor Store who will usually sign a long term lease. This store is a draw that will help keep the smaller stores full of tenants, who will pay higher rents because the Anchor Store does the advertising effectively for them. Add a few more Anchor type stores and a lot more small stores and we call this a Mall.

Industrial Properties are also popular investments. Within this category there are warehouses which may store goods for long or short periods of time. Distribution warehouses are used to divide goods and re-distribute them in a short period of time. There are factories where parts are created and manufacturing buildings where various parts may be assembled. Other manufacturing buildings may be used to create or produce new products. R&D buildings, Research and Development, may be a combination of manufacturing and warehouse space. Generally the tenants in these building seek longer term leases, making their "stability" attractive to investors.

Many products have gotten smaller. In many areas the older, larger industrial building is too big for most tenants. Investors have bought these buildings, a 50,000 SF building may today be divided into ten 5,000 SF units creating an investment property.

"Flex" buildings as they are called are not really a type of building but rather refers to zoning. Large buildings sitting dormant due to lack of big tenants are not good for the owner or for the community. In some areas these building are rezoned to allow multiple uses; for example part of the building may be a retail showroom, part leased for office and part for warehouse use.

Multi Family buildings can range in size from 2-4 residential units, generally considered as residential property to large apartment complexes of 250 units or more, over 5 units are considered commercial properties. The owner may live in one of the apartments but in most cases they do not. It is common however in larger apartment buildings to have a superintendant living in the building. Usually their apartment is rent free – part of their compensation package. They are responsible for the day-to-day maintenance of the building and units. It is also common in the larger units to have a Management Company responsible for the billing and collection of rents, overall repairs and maintenance and leasing of units that become available. The duties and fees paid to a Management Company can vary depending upon the agreed contract.

Multi Use properties are very common in our "main street" areas. Typically you will see a group of buildings built adjacent to each other. Each will have a store or office on the ground floor and several apartments on the second or third floor. These buildings are often called **Taxpayers**. The term originated as towns and villages were being developed in the early1900"s. The owner would operate their business on the ground floor, live in one of the upstairs apartments and the income from the other apartment(s) would literally be used to pay the real estate taxes on the building. Today one may buy the property as an investment and put your business there but they will probably live elsewhere, utilizing the apartment income to reduce their expenses.

We also see larger multi use buildings today with several retail or office units on the ground floor and many floors of apartment units above. In many of our cities this **Mixed Use Zoning,** also being referred to as **Smart Growth** communities, is being encouraged today, with high rise buildings having a couple of floors of retail, followed by several floors of office or even hotel rooms with additional floors of apartments or condominiums above that.

Land may be purchased as an investment to be developed at a future date. Over time the value may appreciate.

Land may also be leased creating a cash flow for the owner. In the case of a land lease it is the responsibility of the tenant to build their own building at their expense. Consequently a land lease is typically written for a 49 year term or longer; previously most were written for a 99 year term.

Chapter 4: Basic Investment Concepts

Commercial Buildings – Square Footage

Commercial real estate is generally talked about in terms of size being described as square footage [length or depth multiplied by width equals square footage]. It is usually priced by a cost per square foot (PSF). This PSF pricing is used in either leasing or sale.

For example:
The building measures 25' in front and is 40' deep, thus being a 1,000 SF building.
(25' x 40' = 1,000 Square Feet)

In leasing, if the rent to be charged is $15 PSF (per square foot), the annual cost to lease the space is $15,000.
(1,000 SF x $15 PSF = $15,000).

If the property were being sold for $150,000 the cost per foot would be $150.
($150,000 ÷ 1,000 SF = $150 PSF)

Another common term is **Frontage.** This refers to the portion or side of the property (typically the width) that has the main street exposure. In this example the frontage is 25 feet.

Lease verses Buy Concepts

Owning a business may require one to have a store to sell the goods from, an office to operate out of or a place to manufacture or store products in. Choices to acquire the necessary space for the business are to lease (rent) space in a building, or to buy a building large enough for the needs of the business or to buy a building larger than needed that has income from other tenants.

One's financial capability will also be part of this decision. Leasing space makes the cost of rent an expense against the income from the business and affords no investment opportunity.

Buying a building just large enough to house your business will require the purchase money or at least a down payment if financed. From an investment point of view if the building were purchased for all cash the saving in rent that would otherwise have to be paid could be considered as the return on the investment or the cash flow. There is also the possibility that over time the investment would appreciate.

For example:

A client needs a 1,000 SF to operate a shoe store. Consider a choice between renting a store of 1,000 SF at a cost of $15 PSF; annual rent being $15,000; or in comparison purchasing a small 1,000 SF building for $150,000 all cash.

If they purchased the building it could be considered that the consequential rent savings of $15,000 could be looked at as a **Return on the Investment (ROI)** of 10%.

$$\frac{\$15,000}{\$150,000} \quad = \quad .10 \quad\quad 10\%$$

In addition the building has future appreciation potential.

But, realistically, buying the building may also create other operating expenses the owner must pay for: real estate taxes, insurance, costs of utilities, repairs and maintenance. **Buying a building larger than needed would produce income from other tenants that may offset some of these costs and reduce the rent they would otherwise have to pay for the space they occupy.** Also some of these operating expenses could be **passed through** to the other tenants in the negotiating of their leases.

To illustrate, we will expand the above building example to include a second floor with two apartments, and add owner's expenses.

The ground floor of the building is 1,000 SF, which the buyer will occupy for their business. On the second floor are two apartments which rent for $500 per month each. The owner provides heat to the building, which costs $150 a month, the tenants each have separate electric meters and pay their own electric expenses. The owner pays the real estate taxes of $6,000 per year and pays insurance costs of $1,200 per year. In this case the building is purchased for $180,000.

The return on this investment can be looked at as a rate of return based on the actual investment and annual cash flow, or in terms of how much lower the cost of "renting" the space for their business will be as a result of the income from the other tenants.

Advantage of buying verses leasing
Basic financial analysis focuses on the annual results of an investment. To determine cash flow values are calculated in components of income and owner's expenses. **All figures used in analysis are annualized.**

Income:

Apartment A	$500 mo. X 12 months = $6,000 year
Apartment B	$500 mo. X 12 months = $6,000 year
Total Annual Income	$12,000

Expenses (owner's):

Heat	$150 mo. X 12 months = $1,800 year
RE Taxes	$6,000 year
Insurance	$1,200 year
Total Operating Expenses	$9,000

Income	$12,000
Less Expenses	-$9,000
Cash Flow	$3,000

Here we are considering the advantage of purchasing the building verses renting the store. The buyer was prepared to pay $15,000 a year in rent. If buying the building, the rent they would have had to pay is now reduced by the "profit" of $3,000. Effective rent is reduced to $12,000. The advantage of purchase being a 20% reduction in rent expense, plus the tax benefits of real estate ownership (to be discussed in a future chapter) and appreciation potential.

Pure Investments

The concepts and formulas you have been introduced to may be applied to investment properties of varying sizes. Consider the last example but with a tenant leasing the ground floor. In this case the analysis would appear as follows:

Income:

Ground Floor Tenant   1,000 SF X $15 PSF = $15,000 year

Apartment A $500 mo. X 12 months = $6,000 year

Apartment B $500 mo. X 12 months = $6,000 year

Total Annual Income $27,000

Expenses (owner's):

Heat $150 mo. X 12 months = $1,800 year

RE Taxes $6,000 year

Insurance $1,200 year

Total Operating Expenses $9,000

Income less Expenses equals Net Operating Income (NOI)

Income $27,000

Less Expenses   -$9,000

Net Operating Income $18,000

This is a Key Formula for investment properties:

Gross Operating Income

Less: Owners Operating Expenses

Equals: Net Operating Income

To determine the **ROI - Return on Investment** rate (percentage) we use the following formula:

$$\underline{\textbf{Income}} \quad = \quad \textbf{Rate}$$
$$\textbf{Value}$$

In this case the Income is the NOI; the Value is the amount (cost) of the investment and the Rate is the percentage rate of return on the investment.

$$\underline{\$18{,}000} \quad = \quad .10 \qquad 10\% \ ROI$$
$$\$180{,}000$$

As a pure investment this property would be producing a 10% return on the amount invested. The investment was $180,000 (the cost of the building). At the end of the year, after reconciling the income and expenses, what remains is a profit of $18,000.

Part3
Financial Analysis

Chapter 5: Income Analysis

A **Pro forma** of a property is a financial analysis that reflects the current year or multiple years <u>expected</u> financial performance of the property. This is also referred to as the **Operating Statement** or the **Income and Expense Statement.** The Pro forma has two primary components, Income and Expenses. In this chapter we will examine the components of "income", analyzing several types of income and adjustments, which will conclude with an "Income Summary" generally referred to as the **Gross Operating Income.**

To calculate the Gross Operating Income we will consider the four components of income:

Potential Rental Income

Additional Tenant Income

Less Vacancy and Credit Loss Adjustment

Other Building Income

Potential Rental Income

To begin the **Potential Rental Income (PRI)** of the property is determined. This figure reflects the property potential **as if every possible rental area were leased**. Actual leases will show current rent from actual tenants; then a projection of potential rent for temporally unoccupied space is included (realistically based upon current market conditions).

Example:

The property is composed of a five store strip center; each store is 1,000 SF and the tenants pay $16 PSF in rent.

A video store occupies 2 store fronts, one store is a pizza parlor, one a card store and the other store is vacant.

Store	Space Occupied	Rent PSF	Annual Rent
Video store	2,000 SF	$16	$32,000
Pizza	1,000 SF	$16	$16,000
Card shop	1,000 SF	$16	$16,000
Vacant store	1,000 SF	$16*	$16,000
Potential Rental Income			**$80,000**

*The rent for the vacant store has been projected based upon current market conditions. In this case it is assumed that if all the other tenants are paying $16 PSF a new tenant for this store will pay the same.

Additional Tenant Income

Owners sometimes **pass through** certain expenses to tenants; which they pay as **additional rent**. For example: an office building that has 25 tenants. The building has one source of power (one electric meter) and the owner passes through the cost of electricity to the tenants. The owner may examine the electric bill and determine the cost of electricity for the building per square foot. Then bill each tenant that amount for each square foot they occupy as additional rent. In quoting the tenants cost of the space an example would be, the rent is $25.00 per square foot plus $2.25 per square foot for electric.

Another way this cost may be passed through is based on the percentage of the building each tenant occupies. In their lease this may be referred to as paying their **proportionate share** of the buildings electric or utility costs. If they occupy 10% of the building each month they would be billed for 10% of the electric costs.

Another typical pass through is known as **CAM Charges (Common Area Maintenance).** For the convenience of all the tenants the landlord may contract services of various vendors. The combined costs of all these services are divided by the total square footage of the building. The tenants are then billed for their proportionate share of these expenses.

CAM Charges Example:

The landlord of a 25,000 SF office building has service contracts with the following vendors:

Service	Annual Cost
Rubbish Collection	$24,000
Window Washing	$12,000
Elevator Maintenance	$6,000
Cleaning	$18,000
Landscaping	$6,000
Security	$9,000
Total Cost	$75,000

This is now divided by the size of the building giving a proportionate cost per square foot.

$$\frac{\$75,000}{25,000 \text{ SF}} = \$3 \text{ PSF CAM Charge}$$

Each tenant will be billed $3. PSF as additional rent for CAM charges.

Another additional rent item may be a result of real estate taxes being passed through to the tenants. Depending on the lease negotiations a tenant may be responsible to pay the entire (or their proportionate share) of the property real estate taxes. Another clause that may be used in a lease is a **"Tax Escalation Clause" also called a "Tax Stop" or referred to as "RET Over Base" (Real Estate Taxes Over Base).** In this case at the time of lease signing the current real estate taxes for the building or **Base Taxes** will be stated in the lease. It is the responsibility of the landlord to pay the base taxes. If however the real estate taxes on the building increase after lease signing the tenant will be responsible to pay their proportionate share of the increase.

Tax Escalation Example:

A tenant enters into a lease of 4,000 SF in a large office building that totals 100,000 SF in size. The lease has a Tax Escalation Clause; the tenant is occupying 4% of the building. Upon lease signing the Base Taxes are defined as $350,000. Two years later the real estate taxes are increased by 3%. The tenant is responsible for their proportionate share of the tax increase.

Base Taxes	$350,000	
Tax Increase (to the building)	$10,500	(3% increase)
Tenants share (4%)	$420	
($10,500 X .04 = $420)		

The tenant will have additional rent to pay of $420. based on the Tax Escalation Clause in their lease. This may not seem like a lot of money but if your area has relatively consistent tax increases the cumulative total could add up quickly. From a landlords perspective if all the tenants in the building have Tax Escalation Clauses in their leases the entire tax increase is passed through to the tenants, hence the term **Tax Stop.**

These are examples of "additional rent" items. In examining the building's performance these monies need to be added to the Potential Rental Income of the building.

Vacancy Adjustments

To develop an accurate picture of the performance of a property consideration must be given to the possibility of **Vacancy.** Even if a building is currently fully occupied a vacancy adjustment is appropriate to the building Pro forma. It addresses the possibility that a tenant may leave and create a vacancy.

The vacancy adjustment reduces the property income and its value; sellers may and to use a low or no vacancy adjustment in their financials. Buyers must be very realistic in their pro forma as this affects the NOI.

Vacancy – A portion or entire space without tenancy for a <u>period of time</u>. From an investor's point of view, potential vacancy is measured as an expense adjustment to the Potential Rental Income, including rent and any additional tenant income. It is calculated in percentage terms, and then converted to dollars that are subtracted from the Potential Rental Income.

As an illustration if we had 10,000 SF office building with average rental charges of $20. PSF; the potential rental income would be $200,000.
(10,000 SF X $20. PSF = $200,000).

The landlord also charges the tenants additional rent for CAM Charges, $2.00 PSF.
(10,000 SF X $2. PSF = $20,000).

It may be anticipated that some space in the building would be vacant for some period of time during the year. For this example assume a vacancy rate of 5%. Income must now be adjusted. The vacancy amount in dollars is calculated by multiplying the vacancy rate by the total rental income from the tenants.
($220,000 X .05 [5%] = $11,000)

The resulting dollar figure is subtracted from the total rental income yielding the **Effective Rental Income** (consider this a sub-total).

Potential Rental Income	$200,000
Additional Income from Tenants	$20,000
Total Tenant Income	$220,000
Less: Vacancy Adjustment 5%	-$11,000
Effective Rental Income	$209,000

Note: the vacancy adjustment is taken on all tenant income, potential rental income plus any additional income from the tenants.

Calculating the Vacancy Adjustment Percentage

The question becomes what is the correct percentage adjustment for vacancy? This will require reality examinations of market and building conditions. If space becomes vacant how long will it take before the landlord replaces the tenant and **starts receiving rent again** for that space? Market conditions give a strong clue to how long it may take to get a new tenant. If you have a store available in your strip center and there are other stores available in every other strip center in town – how long will it take to rent your store? If there are no other vacancies in town – how long will it take? Is your rental goal price **competitive** to what else is available?

Other considerations could affect the time it will take before the landlord actually receives rent. What if the former tenant was a card store but the new tenant will be a hair salon, requiring plumbing work to operate. There could be down time for **construction** or obtaining zoning or building approval. In some cases to attract a stronger tenant a **concession** or free rent period may have to be offered. This free rent period is also referred to as an **abatement** of rent. In calculating a vacancy adjustment all these possibilities must be considered.

One needs to anticipate how long it will take to replace the tenant and start receiving rent, considering "the three C's" competition, the possibility of construction, and the possibility of a concession. **Once the amount of time required to again receive rent is determined the vacancy percentage adjustment may be calculated.**

Example:

Assume you own a five store strip center, each store is 1,000 SF and tenants pay $15 PSF rent. If a store becomes vacant you anticipate, based on current market conditions that it will take six months to lease the store and start receiving rent. Given this situation what is the vacancy adjustment rate?

This is calculated as follows:

Potential Rental Income	$75,000
(1,000 SF X $15 PSF X 5 stores)	
Vacant Space 1,000 SF	
Annual Rent (1,000 SF X $15 PSF = $15,000)	$15,000
Monthly Rent (Annual rent divided by 12 months)	$1,250
Potential Lost Income (Monthly rent times 6 months vacancy)	$7,500

Key Formula:

$$\frac{\text{Potential Lost Income}}{\text{Potential Rental Income}} = \text{Vacancy Adjustment Rate}$$

$$\frac{\$7,500}{\$75,000} = .10 \quad \text{10\% Vacancy Adjustment}$$

As another example, if you had ten stores in the strip center all else being equal.

Potential Rental Income	$150,000
(1,000 SF X $15 PSF X 10 stores)	
Vacant Space 1,000 SF	
Annual Rent (1,000 SF X $15 PSF = $15,000)	$15,000
Monthly Rent (Annual rent divided by 12 months)	$1,250
Potential Lost Income (Monthly rent times 6 months vacancy)	$7,500

$$\frac{\text{Potential Lost Income}}{\text{Potential Rental Income}} = \text{Vacancy Adjustment Rate}$$

$$\frac{\$7,500}{\$150,000} = .05 \quad \text{5\% Vacancy Adjustment}$$

Remember the vacancy expense rate requires a "realty check" which may include examining vacancies in similar buildings in the area.

The complete term for this category is **Vacancy and Credit Loss Adjustment.** Credit Losses are usually grouped into this calculation. **Credit Losses** are rent lost due to non-payment by the tenant. The tenant may "move out overnight" or declare bankruptcy. Credit losses are part of the vacancy contingency.

Important note: In financial analysis **Vacancy and Credit Losses** are deducted as part of the income analysis section of the pro forma.

In constructing a pro forma what has been discussed so far would appear as follows:

Potential Rental Income

Additional Income from Tenants

Less: Vacancy and Credit Losses

Effective Rental Income

Other Building Income

There is another category of income to a building that has nothing to do with the tenants and is therefore not subject to an adjustment for vacancy. The building itself may serve as a source of income. For example an advertising billboard may be mounted on the roof or side of the building. Often there is an opportunity to place antennas or satellite dishes on the roof by a phone or beeper company for a fee. In apartment houses the laundry room operation may serve as an additional source of revenue to the building. Even vending machines can produce additional revenue for the owner. These sources of income to the building need to be included in the income analysis. The total revenue is added to the Effective Rental Income and the result is the **Gross Operating Income.**

Recap

A complete income analysis may appear as follows:

Potential Rental Income

Additional Income from Tenants

Less: Vacancy and Credit Losses

Effective Rental Income (sub-total)

Plus: Other Building Income

Results in: Gross Operating Income

Income Analysis Example

You own a five store strip center. Each store is 1,000 SF and tenants pay $15 PSF rent. You provide services for the benefit of all the tenants (rubbish pick up, landscaping, and parking lot cleaning), and you bill each tenant CAM Charges of $2 PSF. An analysis of market conditions determines a 10% vacancy rate is an appropriate contingent adjustment. Your building backs up to a Rail Road track and consequently an advertising company pays you $500 per month for a billboard on the rear of your building. What is the Gross Operating Income of your property?

Step 1 – Determine the Potential Rental Income

Fives stores, each 1,000 SF, each paying $15 PSF. The annual rent from each store is $15,000.
(1,000 SF X $15 = $15,000)

With 5 stores the Potential Rental Income (PRI) is $75,000.
($15,000 income per store multiplied by 5 stores = $75,000)

Step 2 – Determine if there is any other income from the tenants.

In this case the tenants pay $2 PSF in CAM Charges. The five stores total 5,000 SF; therefore the additional income from tenants is $10,000.
(5,000 SF building X $2 PSF CAM = $10,000)

Step 3 – Calculate the Vacancy and Credit Loss adjustment.

An analysis of market conditions concluded that in this area at this time a 10% adjustment would be appropriate. **All the income from the tenants must be considered.** The Potential Rental Income and the Additional Income from Tenants are added together; then 10% of this amount will be subtracted from the total as the Vacancy adjustment.

Potential Rental Income	$75,000
Additional Income	$10,000
Total Income	$85,000
Vacancy Adjustment 10%	-$8,500
Effective Rental Income	$76,500

Step 4 – Consider any income to the building from sources other than the tenants.

In this case an advertising company pays for billboard space at a rate of $500. per month.

*Important Note: All figures in analysis must be annualized.

Other Building Income   +$6,000
($500 X 12 months= $6,000)

Step 5 – Determine the Gross Operating Income (GOI)

Adding Other Building Income to the Effective Rental Income produces the Gross Operating Income for the property.

Summary Follows:

Potential Rental Income	$75,000
Plus Additional Income from Tenants	$10,000
Less: Vacancy and Credit Losses	-$8,500
(10% of the Total Income $85,000)	
Effective Rental Income	$76,500
Other Building Income	+$6,000
Gross Operating Income	$82,500

The Gross Operating Income of a property has taken into consideration the total potential income of the tenants, realistically made adjustments for possible vacancy and included any other revenue sources from the building.

Chapter 6: Owners Operating Expenses

The next component in analyzing the financial performance of a property is the expenses that are paid by the owner or landlord.

Who pays for what expenses of a building are defined in the leases between the landlord and tenants. (Types of leases will be discussed in a further chapter.) In analyzing the building or property one is only concerned with the **expenses paid by the owner.**

Often when one is considering purchase of a property and Income and Expense Statement will be supplied by the owner. This may have been prepared for purposes other than selling the building and may contain items that are not appropriate to the analysis of the building itself.

If a corporation owns the building the Income and Expense Statement may reflect other expenses of that corporation. Some statements show tax benefits to the owner that may not apply to a new buyer. For example the current owner may have financed the building with a mortgage and the statement shows a deduction for interest expense. A new buyer may pay all cash and have no such deduction. **In a pro forma Annual Debt Service (the repayment of the mortgage loan) is not included as a building expense in determining Net Operating Income.** Statements provided by owners must be carefully analyzed to be sure only actual building expenses are considered in the financial analysis of the property.

A typical list of property expenses may include:

Real Estate Taxes

In some States Personal Property Taxes

Insurance

Accounting

Legal

Permits or Licenses

Utilities

Advertising

Supplies

Contract Services

(**routine** weekly, monthly or seasonal services. i.e. rubbish collection, window washing, cleaning, elevator maintenance, landscaping, snow removal).

Building Employees Expenses

(This could include salary, benefits, payroll taxes, worker's compensation, etc.)

Management Expenses

Reserves

Any other actual building or property expenses

A buyer will verify all income and expenses presented by the owner. Usually during the **Due Diligence** period of a purchase contract the buyer, their attorney or their accountant will examine all the leases, verify the income and require copies of bills to confirm stated expenses.

Care must be taken when examining the expenses of a building. What are in fact the expenses of the current owner may not be the future expenses of the buyer. As an illustration, the current owner bought a three-year insurance policy for the building and is paying $5,000 annually. However, since the policy was purchased insurance costs have gone up. To insure the building today will cost the buyer $6,500 per year. This would of course change the expense costs of the building and the potential profitability.

"Repair and Maintenance" Contingency Expenses also referred to as a "Reserve for Replacement" or "Replacement Reserve".

Contingency expenses are best thought of as reserves for irregular, unexpected or emergency events. There is an important distinction between <u>routine regular expenses</u> and contingency repair and maintenance expenses.

Normal regular expenses are listed under the "Contract Service" category previously described. A prudent owner will also set aside funds for an emergency like a roof leak or roof replacement, repair of the building heating system, structural damage, parking lot repair or other unexpected events. This fund is considered an expense of the building and is listed under the category "Repair and Maintenance"

The question that arises is what is the appropriate amount of money to set aside? This is a reality question. What is the age and condition of the building? A relatively new building that may have existing guarantees on the roof and heating systems would require a lesser reserve than perhaps a building that's 30 years old and still has its original roof. **Buyers need to have an Engineer inspect a building they are considering purchasing.**

Another guideline to determining the amount of money to set aside for Repair and Maintenance contingency is what responsibilities the owner has under the terms of the lease. A building may have a single tenant who is responsible for all repairs to the building. Or on the other extreme the landlord may be responsible for everything!

As a general "rule of thumb" Replacement Reserves are usually calculated at 5% to 10% of the buildings income. Unfortunately some consider the "buildings income" to be the Potential Rental Income and others use the Gross Operating Income for their calculations, and in some cases a fixed fee is used. Care must be taken in determining a realistic figure no matter how it is calculated.

This is an expense that ultimately will affect the projected profit of the building. Often the owner and buyer will have a different perspective on the value of this category.

Building Management

Another expense category is Building Management, sometimes also referred to as Off Site Management. This may become another issue between the owner and buyers perspective of the building expenses. The owner may manage the building themselves, where the buyer employees a real estate broker or management company to do so.

As another "rule of thumb" smaller buildings perhaps with up to 5 or 6 tenants may be considered owner manageable and this expense would not be included in the pro forma. Larger buildings would need to expense Building Management.

Management contracts and costs vary significantly based on the defined duties and the local market conditions. A range for management services may be 3% to 6% of the tenant income. Typically this is paid based on the potential building rent or actual rent collected.

For analysis purposes the value sited as Potential Rental Income is generally used to calculate this expense and 5% is a typical fee used in the pro forma.

On the low end of services the manager may "baby sit" the building. In the event of a problem the tenant calls the manager who calls the repair or Service Company from a vendors list provided by the owner, then inspects the work and authorizes payment of the bill. A more comprehensive contract could have the manager collecting the rents, paying all the bills and sending the owner monthly reports and payments. Some management contracts also provide leasing services, negotiations of lease renewals and/or leasing of vacant space.

Net Operating Income (NOI)

Once all of the owner's annual expenses of the property or building have been determined they are totaled and referred to as the **Total Operating Expenses.**

In the previous chapter, Income Analysis we learned that the owner may pass though some expenses to the tenants as additional rent. (i.e. CAM Charges, Utility costs, Taxes or Tax Escalations) Even if this is done the owner will actually be paying these expenses and these costs must be reflected in the expense section of the pro forma.

The final step in this analysis is to subtract the Total Operating Expenses from the Gross Operating Income to determine the Net Operating Income of the building or property.

The **Pro Forma** or **Operating Statement** shows the detailed income and expenses of the building or property and concludes with the Net Operating Income. This is reflective of the current years projected income of the property.

Key Formula:

Potential Rental Income

Additional Income from Tenants

Less: Vacancy and Credit Losses

Effective Rental Income (sub-total)

Plus: Other Building Income

Results in: Gross Operating Income

Less: Owners Operating Expenses

Equals: Net Operating Income (NOI)

To assist you in analyzing investment properties I have developed the form on the next page.

Investment Properties: Financial Analysis

Address: _____

Type of Property: _____ **Size:** _____

Enter all figures as annual totals.

Notes and Calculations

Tenant Income:
    Actual Rent:
    Projected Rent:
    Additional Rent
      CAM:
      Taxes:
      Utilities:
      Other:
Total Tenant Income:
Minus: Vacancy Contingency
Adjustment   (_____ %)
Adjusted Tenant Income:
Other Property Income:
Total Gross Income:

Operating Expenses (Paid by Owner)

Real Estate Taxes:
Insurance:
Utilities:

    _____
    _____
    _____

Contract Services:

    _____
    _____
    _____
    _____
    _____

Accounting:
Legal:
Other Professional Services:
Payroll:
Management (_____ %):
Repair & Maintenance (_____ %):
Other:

    _____
    _____

Total Operating Expenses:
Net Operating Income (NOI):
CAP Rate: _____ %

Market Value: _____

49

Case Study – Investment Analysis

Determine the Net Operating Income of a small Office Building consisting of four rental units with a Gross Leasable Area (GLA) of 5,000 SF. The rent roll follows:

Suite	Square Footage	Rent PSF	Annual Rent
101	2,000	$26	$52,000
102	1,000	$24	$24,000
103	1,000	$25	$25,000
104 (Vacant)	1,000	$24	$24,000

All tenants pay $1 PSF CAM charges

Landlord's Expenses:

Fuel Oil	$500 per month
Landscaping	$550 per year
Electricity (signs)	$100 per month
Insurance	$5,000 a year
Snow Removal	$350 per year
Rubbish Removal	$200 per month
Accountant	$500 per year
Property Taxes	$25,000 annually

The landlord rarely has vacancies but uses 5% vacancy contingency in his financial statements. He manages the center himself. The owner put 5% of the gross income a year into an emergency repair and maintenance fund. There are no other expenses. What is the NOI?

A completed calculation of the Office Building using the financial Analysis Form follows. Tenant Income consists of actual rents, projected rents (for any temporally unoccupied space) and any additional (pass through) rent. This total is then adjusted for the possibility of vacancy. If there is any non-tenant income to the building (antennas, billboards, vending machines etc.) this is added in resulting in the Total Gross Income.

In this example the actual rent totals $101,000, projected rent is $24,000 and additional rent in the form of passed through CAM Charges is $5,000 ($1 per SF; building totals 5,000 SF); when totaled, this is $130,000. A vacancy adjustment is calculated based upon 5% of the potential income, $6,500 ($130,000 X .05). This is subtracted from the Total Tenant Income yielding a Adjusted Tenant Income of $123,500. In this building there is a roof antenna paying $500 a month; $6,000 per year. This is added to the Adjusted Tenant Income providing a Total Gross Income of $129,500.

Using the form as a checklist the owner operating expenses are calculated. All figures must be annualized. Real estate taxes are $25,000; insurance is $5,000; fuel oil is $500 per month, ($500 X 12 months) entered as $6,000 annual expense; electric $1,200 year ($100 X 12); Rubbish Removal $2,400 annually ($200 per month); Landscaping $550 year; Snow Removal $350 year; and accounting $500 per year.

Note some of these expenses are passed through to the tenants in the form of CAM Charges, but the owner must still pay the bills, so they are listed as expenses on the analysis form.

A Maintenance and Repair (emergency, contingency) fund is established, based on the property being in good condition 5% of the Gross Income ($129,500) is used $6,475.

The Total Operating Expenses $47,475 are deducted from the Total Gross Income $129,500 yielding an NOI (Net Operating Income) of $82,025.

Investment Properties: Financial Analysis

Address: _____Main Street_____

Type of Property: _____Office Building_____ Size: _____5.000 SF_____

Enter all figures as annual totals.

Notes and Calculations

Tenant Income:

Actual Rent:	___$101,000_____	_____
Projected Rent:	____$24,000_____	__1,000SF at $24 PSF_____
Additional Rent		
CAM:	_____$5,000_____	__$1 per SF_____
Taxes:		
Utilities:		
Other:		
Total Tenant Income:	___$130,000_____	
Minus: Vacancy Contingency		
Adjustment (___5___%)	____-$6,500_____	
Adjusted Tenant Income:	__ $123,500_____	
Other Property Income:	____ $6,000_____	_Antenna $500 per month__
Total Gross Income:	__$129,500_____	

Operating Expenses (Paid by Owner)

Real Estate Taxes:	___ $25,000_____	
Insurance:	____ $5,000_____	
Utilities:		
__Fuel Oil_____	____ $6,000_____	__$500 per month_____
__Electric_____	____ $1,200_____	__$100 per month (sign) ___
Contract Services:		
__Rubbish Removal____	____$2,400_____	__$200 per month_____
__Landscaping_____	_____$550_____	
__Snow Removal_____	_____$350_____	
Accounting:	_____$500_____	
Legal:		
Other Professional Services:		
Payroll:		
Management (_____%):		
Repair & Maintenance (___5__%):	____$6,475_____	__5% of Gross Income____
Other:		
Total Operating Expenses:	___ $47,475_____	
Net Operating Income (NOI):	___ $82,025_____	
CAP Rate: _____%		Market Value: _____

Chapter 7 – Determining Value

There are three primary methods used to determine the value of a building or property: **Income Approach**, **Comparable Sales** method and the **Cost Approach**. Other methods include the Gross Rent Multiplier and utilizing Internal Rate of Return (IRR) and Net Present Value (NPV) approaches. Value is generally determined based upon what a building is worth today. However, some investors will project cash flows and value in the future in determining what they will pay for a property. We will examine this, the Internal Rate of Return and Net Present Value approaches in Chapter 10.

Putting aside the methods of calculating value, the real value of a building or property is determined by what a buyer is willing to pay for it. Some will pay more for a specific building or desired location.

Income Approach to Valuation

It is important to have an understanding of this approach, which is one of the factors used by financial institutions (banks) to determine how much they will loan on an investment property.

The **Net Operating Income (NOI)** of the property is the basis of this calculation. Earlier it was learned that; **Income less Expense equals NOI**. Previously the components of income and expense were explored. A building's pro forma can be now summarized:

Gross Operating Income
Less: Total (Owner's) Operating Expenses
Equals: Net Operating Income

To determine value based on the income approach requires a desired rate of return; a **Return on Investment (ROI).** How much is one willing to pay for a building if they want a specific return on their investment? In dollars the return on the investment is the Net Operating Income. The ROI shows the return as a percentage of profit,

Example:

A 10% (.10) return is desired on the investment. Consideration is given to buying a building all cash that has an NOI of $50,000. What can be paid for the building to accomplish this goal?

A formula is used for this calculation.

$$\frac{\textbf{Income}}{\textbf{Rate}} = \textbf{Value}$$

Specifically:

$$\frac{\textbf{Net Operating Income}}{\textbf{Desired Rate of Return}} = \textbf{Value}$$

$$\frac{\textbf{\$50,000 NOI}}{\textbf{.10}} = \textbf{\$500,000}$$

If one pays $500,000, all cash for the building at the end of the year after reconciling the income and expenses, the NOI will be $50,000, yielding the desired 10% Return on Investment (ROI).

The previous formula is interchangeable and can also be used to calculate the rate; if two components are known the third can be solved for.

$$\underline{\text{Income}} = \text{Rate}$$
$$\text{Value}$$

The formula may be applied this way to answer these questions. How has the investment performed? What is the Rate of Return? If we divide the Net Operating Income by the price or value we determine the Return on Investment (ROI).

$$\underline{\$50,000 \text{ NOI}} = .10 \quad 10\% \text{ Rate of Return}$$
$$\$500,000 \text{ Price}$$

Capitalization Rate (CAP Rate)

In order to value investment properties in any market place a **Capitalization Rate** is used. Determining a CAP Rate is a complex mathematical process the takes into consideration local market conditions (supply and demand), local economic conditions (interest rates) and other conditions of loans (down payment percentages).

Since much of the data used to formulate a CAP Rate is local in nature Capitalization Rates will vary in different locations. Generally CAP Rates will be posted in regional financial newspapers and may also be found on the Internet sites of such publications. Another source to find local CAP Rates would be Commercial Mortgage Brokers.

From a practical point of view a CAP Rate can be looked at as a desired "profit percentage" for an investor.

It is based upon the premise that a correlation exists between the income a property produces and its value. By using a CAP Rate a Market Value can be determined.

As loans to purchase investment properties are applied for, the financial institutions will see the income and expense statement, NOI and agreed purchase price of these sales. Dividing the NOI by the purchase price shows the percentage return on investment for that transaction. Patterns become apparent in a given area, reflecting an acceptable "profit percentage" by local buyers. This is effectively the CAP Rate.

Note CAP Rates vary in different markets and change often.

The question, "What is the property worth?" can now be answered by applying the **Capitalization (CAP) Rate Formula**.

Key Formula

NOI divided by the CAP Rate equals Market Value

Net Operating Income = Market Value
Capitalization Rate

Example:

A building is determined to have a NOI of $68,500. The local CAP Rate is 7.5%. What is the market value of the building?

$$\frac{\text{NOI}}{\text{CAP Rate}} = \text{Market Value}$$

$$\frac{\$68,500.}{.075} = \$913,333.$$

The Market Value of this building is $913,333.

How is the investor doing on their investment?

This is illustrated by reversing the formulas on this examples. The property is purchased for $913,333 all cash; at the end of the year the NOI is $68,500. What is the investor's **Return on Investment (ROI)?**

$$\frac{\text{Income}}{\text{Value}} = \text{Rate}$$

$$\frac{\$68,500 \text{ NOI}}{\$913,333 \text{ Price}} = .075 \quad \text{7.5\% Rate of Return}$$

The return on the investment, based on the annual cash flow is 7.5%.

What if the CAP Rate were 6%?

$$\frac{\text{NOI}}{\text{CAP Rate}} = \text{Market Value}$$

$$\frac{\$68,500.}{.06} = \$1,141,666.$$

Now the Market Value of the building would be $1,141,666.

> **Important Concept:**
>
> **As the Cap Rate goes down the Value goes up.**

If more money were to be paid to buy the property the return on the investment would be less.

The property is purchased for $1,141,666 all cash: at the end of the year the NOI is $68,500.

$$\frac{\text{Income}}{\text{Value}} = \text{Rate}$$

$$\frac{\$68,500 \text{ NOI}}{\$1,141,666 \text{ Price}} = .06 \qquad \textbf{6\% Rate of Return}$$

The higher the price paid the less percentage return on the investment.

This rate of return, in all cash purchases, is referred to as the **Return on Investment (ROI).**

When selling a property this return, based on the asking price, is referred to as the CAP Rate.

For Sale: Office Investment Property
Price: $1,150,000.
CAP: 6%

One further point on CAP Rates, in addition to varying geographically they may vary by type of property within a market. i.e. Office buildings 7.5% CAP, Multi-Family investments 4% CAP Rate. Also they are constantly changing based upon local economic conditions.

Case Study – Office Building

We can now calculate the value of the Small Office Building property we analyzed previously. The NOI was determined to be $82,025. If the prevailing cap rate were 7.5%, the value of the property would be $1,093,667

.

$$\frac{\text{NOI}}{\text{CAP Rate}} = \text{Market Value}$$

$$\frac{\$82,025}{.075} = \$1,093,667$$

Follows is the fully completed Investment Analysis Form.

Investment Properties: Financial Analysis

Address: _____Main Street_____

Type of Property: _____Office Building_____ Size: _____5.000 SF_____

Enter all figures as annual totals.

Notes and Calculations

Tenant Income:

Actual Rent:	___$101,000_____	_____
Projected Rent:	____$24,000_____	__1,000SF at $24 PSF_____
Additional Rent		
CAM:	_____$5,000_____	__$1 per SF_____
Taxes:	_____	_____
Utilities:	_____	_____
Other:	_____	_____
Total Tenant Income:	___$130,000_____	
Minus: Vacancy Contingency		
Adjustment (___5___%)	____-$6,500_____	_____
Adjusted Tenant Income:	__ $123,500_____	
Other Property Income:	____ $6,000_____	_Antenna $500 per month__
Total Gross Income:	___$129,500_____	

Operating Expenses (Paid by Owner)

Real Estate Taxes:	___ $25,000_____	_____
Insurance:	____ $5,000_____	_____
Utilities:		
__Fuel Oil_____	____ $6,000_____	__$500 per month_____
__Electric _____	____ $1,200_____	__$100 per month (sign) ___
_____	_____	_____
_____	_____	_____
Contract Services:		
__Rubbish Removal____	____$2,400_____	___$200 per month_____
__Landscaping_____	____$550	_____
__Snow Removal_____	____$350	_____
_____	_____	_____
_____	_____	_____
Accounting:	____$500	_____
Legal:	_____	_____
Other Professional Services:	_____	_____
Payroll:	_____	_____
Management (_____%):	_____	_____
Repair & Maintenance (___5__%):	____$6,475_____	___5% of Gross Income____
Other:		
_____	_____	_____
_____	_____	_____
Total Operating Expenses:	___ $47,475_____	
Net Operating Income (NOI):	___ $82,025_____	
CAP Rate: ___7.5_____%		Market Value: ____$1,093,667_____

Appraising Properties

Looking at recent history we learned many things. As a result of the economic turmoil in the late 2000's commercial property values dropped 25% - 30% or even more in some areas from 2007 to 2013. As values declined we saw an increase in vacancy percentages and a decrease in rental values. What could space that was leased at $30 PSF in 2007 for 5 years, be rented for when the lease was up in 2012? We may find the rental value at that time was only $25 PSF. Projection the buildings performance for the next five years would show that even though the current operating statement is true, the future Potential Rental Income, based on new tenants must realistically be reduced. Consequently the NOI and Value would need to be reduced.

To value properties today the Income Approach will still be used but further adjustments must be made. Appraisers today are using a blended approach to value properties; looking at the three primary methods of valuation: Income Approach, Comparable Approach and Cost Approach. Today, February, 2018, in most areas values have returned to the pre 2007 levels.

Comparable Approach to Valuation

Another approach to determining the value of investment property is by the use of comparable sales. What have other buildings that are similar in nature recently sold for?

This immediately creates a number of dilemmas. Comparing office buildings, for example, are they really the same construction, image, size with the same amenities? The rental rates of each building can generally give us a clue. A realistic comparison will require each building having similar attributes or making adjustments for differences.

Is it possible to compare similar buildings that vary in size? If the values (prices paid) and the overall square footage of the building are known, one can divide the value by the square footage and determine the price per square foot that was paid. If you determine the average price per square foot that has been paid, this can be applied to the subject property to determine its value.

Example:

Consideration is given to purchasing a building that is 9,500 Square Feet (SF). Data on similar type buildings that have recently sold is obtained but they vary in size. The price per square foot is calculated.

Similar Office Buildings	Comparable A	Comparable B	Comparable C
Price Paid	$1,050,000.	$957,000.	$920,000.
Size: (SF)	10,000	8,700	9,200
Price per Square Foot	$105.	$110.	$100.

The average price paid was $105. per square foot. Applying this to the subject property shows a value of $997,500. (9,500 SF X $105. = $997,500.)

Another adjustment may need to be made for time. If there are not a lot of recent sales, comparisons may be being made to properties that sold six months or a year ago. Have property values in the area increased or decreased during that time? If so the percentage of increase or decrease needs to be adjusted to the sale price of those buildings to value the current building today. Other adjustments may also be needed if the buildings have different construction qualities or designs.

In many areas sale of properties are public records and they may be obtained from the local government. Many real estate firms belong to organizations that provide sales data.

It may also be prudent for a potential buyer to hire an Appraisal firm to value the property.

Comparing in a Declining Market

As a result of the 2008 "Mortgage Meltdown" the banking regulators reactions made it virtually impossible to finance commercial properties from 2008 through December of 2010. At that point the banking regulators relaxed some of their restrictions and loans started to flow again, but with tightened underwriting requirements. Even with that, the banks were still skittish on lending and it was very difficult to get a loan prior to 2013. Consequently, the economic conditions that created a decline in real estate values also produced very little sales activity.

However, as time went on we saw a growing number of properties coming on the market. Pricing became focused on competition. What buildings on the market am I competing with to sell my building? What other properties do the buyers have to choose from and what are those properties priced at? A comparison can be made based on the asking price per square foot of similar properties as was done above for previous sales. Although this is not a definitive valuation it will give an indication of what a current buyer may consider paying for a property. Valuation requires consideration of several methods and ultimately a judgment based on the best available data.

Cost Approach

The cost approach in essence asks the question if one were to buy land and build a new building what would the total cost be. The expense is then compared to the cost of buying an existing building. This will require finding land costs and getting construction estimates. Other adjustments to have a fair comparison may also be needed. A new building may cost more but require less maintenance, perhaps have guarantees on the roof and heating systems. All these things must be evaluated to have a proper comparison of value.

GREEN Buildings

New building and retrofits that are constructed using Green concepts create a new challenge to valuation. The concept of Green is to have a more energy efficient and environmentally beneficial building. The costs of doing so have finally made financial sense. However the initial capital outlay for improvements may be high. Consequently when valuing green buildings we must answer the question, what would be the cost to replicate this building? Generally the cost approach to valuation is used; however the income approach is also applicable. The Green improvements will reduce the operating expenses of the building, which will increase the Net Operating Income of the property making it more valuable. Less tangible but also of significant value will be the improvement of indoor air quality and other working conditions, which increases tenant retention.

Gross Rent Multiplier

Another method of valuing similar type and size properties is by the Gross Rent Multiplier (GRM). A factor (multiple) is developed by dividing the sales price of a building by the gross income (rent) of that property. The gross income of another building is then multiplied by that factor to determine that building's market value.

$$\frac{\textbf{Sales Price}}{\textbf{Gross Rent}} = \textbf{Gross Rent Multiplier}$$

$$\textbf{Gross Rent X GRM} = \textbf{Market Value}$$

This is typically based upon the annual gross rental income but, may also be calculated based on the monthly gross rental income.

Example:

Building A has gross income of $190,000 and sells for $2,000,000. Building B has gross income of $210,000. What is the value of the building B using the Gross Rent Multiplier? Determine the Gross Rent Multiplier for building A.

$$\frac{\text{Sales Price}}{\text{Gross Rent}} = \text{GRM}$$

$$\frac{\$2,000,000 \text{ (Sales Price)}}{\$190,000 \text{ (Gross Income)}} = 10.5263 \text{ GRM}$$

Rounded off the GRM may be stated as 10.5.

Multiply the gross income of building B by the Gross Rent Multiplier.

Gross Rent X GRM = Market Value

$210,000 X 10.5 = $2,205,000

The value of building B is $2,205,000.

When a property is being sold it is sometimes stated that the property is being sold at "X" times the rent roll. This would imply that the Gross Rent Multiplier is being used to value the building.

Example:

The price is $800,000, which is 8 times the rent roll. Dividing the price by the GRM would equal the gross income.

$$\frac{\$800,000 \text{ (Sales Price)}}{8 \quad \text{(GRM)}} = \$100,000. \text{ Gross Income}$$

Another Example;

The price is $800,000, and the GRM is 15.

$$\frac{\$800,000 \text{ (Sales Price)}}{15 \quad \text{(GRM)}} = \$53,333. \text{ Gross Income}$$

Important Concept:

As the GRM increases the gross income in relation to the price is lower. In other words a high GRM indicates a high price as compared to the gross income. Basically, the lower the GRM is, the better the return on the investment.

However the Gross Rent Multiplier, unlike the income approach, does not take into consideration the actual expenses of the buildings, which even with similar buildings can vary significantly. The GRM method does not consider the possibility of vacancy, nor repair and maintenance contingency based on the age and condition of the property. This may lead to problems in securing financing where **banks generally use the income approach to determine value and the amount they lend.**

Chapter 8: Evaluating the Investment Opportunity

We have previously learned to calculate the current years return on a property known as the NOI (Net Operating Income). We may finance the purchase which, depending on loan terms and interest rates, will produce higher or lower returns on that investment.

To make a decision to buy this property or not will now require further evaluation. Will the return on investment grow in the future? Will the property appreciate in value? What are my risks?

Let us begin by looking at the facts. There are a number of tenants, presumably with leases. Key points to analyze:

- How much time remains in those lease obligations?
- What do the leases say – who is responsible for what expenses?
- How much does the rent go up each year?
- Does the tenant have any options to extend the term of the lease?

The answers to most of these questions will be found in a **Lease Extract.** This is a summary of the leases in a building showing the space occupied by each tenant, when the least starts and ends, annual escalations, base rent, additional rent and renewal options (if any). An example follows:

Lease Extract

Five store Strip Center

Tenant	Rentable SF	Current Rent	Additional Rent	Lease Start Date	Lease End Date	Escala -tions	Options
Shoe	2,500	$14	CAM $1.50	Jan. 10 years ago	Dec. current year	2%	None
Pizza	1,250	$18	CAM $2.00	May 4 years ago	May next year	3%	5 year
Cleaner	1,250	$19	CAM $2.00	March 6 years ago	March 4 years from now	4%	10 year
Bank	1,500	$19	CAM $2.00	Jan, 4 years ago	Jan 16 years from now	10% every 5 years	None
Clothing	3,000	$20	CAM $2.00	June 1 year ago	June 9 years from now	4%	2 – 5 year

This immediately shows us any leases that will be expiring soon. Note the Shoe store lease expires at the end of this year and they are paying considerably less than the other tenants are paying now. If they wish to stay their rent will need to be increased to today's market value. Also future escalations will be increased.

How are market conditions? Will we be able to rent that space quickly if the tenant does not renew their lease? Are the annual rent increases (escalations) realistic, keeping up with inflation? What expenses are the landlord responsible for; are any of these costs paid for in part by the tenants? A lot can be learned from the lease extracts; however the entire lease details will need to be reviewed by the buyer or their representative before purchase.

Quality – Stability of Tenants

Yes, you have a contract, a lease that obligates the tenants to pay you rent, but what if they go out of business? In a future Chapter – Leases Clauses, we will review clauses that help protect your property, but prior to purchase, evaluate your risks. What clauses are in their current leases? Who are these tenants?

Nationally known companies are generally considered low risk. They have concern for their reputation. If they close an unsuccessful store or location they will generally continue to pay their rent or reach a mutually satisfactory (buy-out) agreement with the landlord to terminate the lease.

Local businesses as tenants are very common. Ask them how their business is doing and they will generally tell the landlord "great". But is it? There are a few common sense barometers that can give a potential investment buyer, indications of activity (or the lack of it).

Parking lots with office tenants are generally full (or you know how much of the lot is generally occupied). A reduction in the number of cars (employees) could be a hint that a business may be in trouble.

Industrial manufacturers should have a considerable amount of goods coming in or out of the building. What would a lack of truck activity or delivery vans indicate?

You are considering buying a five store strip center, one tenant is a deli that opens at 6:00 am. You park across the street one morning and observe the deli, "that is doing great". It has eleven customers between 6:00 and 8:00 am. Well I guess they could have a lot of deliveries (or not)? How many customers do the other stores have during the day?

A lot can be learned by just observing activity and traffic to and from the property you are considering purchasing.

Spread Sheet Analysis

If we combine the information from the pro forma (current years' analysis of income and expenses) and the lease extracts we can actually project the financial cash flows for future years. Typically this forecasting is done on a basis of a **Five Year Spread Sheet** or a **Ten Year Spread Sheet** for larger properties.

The income calculations reflect the rent escalations for the actual tenants, with projections for replacement rent if the lease expires during the forecasting period.

Here is where **Upside Potential** becomes apparent. There may be a tenant in the building who has been there for a long time and consequently is now paying rent below market value. Their lease may expire in year two or three of the projection period; the space could then be rented for more rent causing a significant increase in income and NOI.

Expenses are projected based upon historic increases for certain items or based on general cost of living increase in that area. Once the projected expenses are charted for each year, the cash flow (NOI) is then calculated for each year.

As we learned earlier the Net Operating Income relates to the value of the property. The spread sheet analysis then gives a good evaluation of future value.

In the following example we see a marked increase in the Potential Rental Income from the current year to Year 2. This probably reflects a tenant who has been in the building a long time and is consequently paying well below market value rent. It appears their lease is up at the end of the current year and a projection is made increasing the rent for that unit to market value in Year 2.

In this example the Real Estate Taxes were grieved and reduced in year 3 and 4, reducing the operating expenses and therefore increasing the NOI.

The current owner financed this property as is reflected by the Annual Debt Service and Cash Flow Before Taxes (CFBT), but as a potential buyer unless you are taking over the Mortgage this is irrelevant information to you. Your focus is the NOI!

If you intend to finance you should calculate your potential Cash-on-Cash return based on today's underwriting requirements and available financial terms.

Spread Sheet: Five-Year Forecast

	Current Year	Year 2	Year 3	Year 4	Year 5
Potential Rental Income	141,750	156,835	160,932	168,013	172,379
Vacancy Adjustment	9,923	10,978	11,265	11,761	12,067
Other Income	6,000	6,000	6,000	6,000	6,000
Gross Operating Income	**137,827**	**151,857**	**155,667**	**162,252**	**166,312**
Expenses:					
Taxes	50,000	50,000	47,500	45,000	45,000
Repair and Maintenance	6,891	7,593	7,783	8,113	8,316
All Other	20,000	20,600	21,218	21,885	22,510
Total Expenses	**76,891**	**78,193**	**76,501**	**74,968**	**75,826**
NOI	60,936	73,664	79,166	87,284	90,486
Debt Service	54,770	54,770	54,770	54,770	54,770
Cash Flow Before Taxes (CFBT)	6,166	18,894	24,396	32,514	35,716

Valuating Investment Properties Today

We learned from the crash in 2008 and the recovery that future projections of a buildings performance may at times decline. Careful examination of leases expiration dates and consideration of current market conditions for new tenants is required.

In valuating these properties a realistic projection of future rent possibilities must be made. Now a spread sheet must be developed showing the projected operating statements for at least the next five years. Your projections could show a consistent increase in cash flows or a reduction in cash flow for a few years followed by an increase as the market conditions rebound.

We will shortly illustrate that using CAP Rate methodology, a value can be determined for future years which may be more realistic that just using the current years operating statement.

As discussed earlier to get a true picture of value today other methods of valuation must also be considered. Traditionally the Comparable Approach is also used, comparing this property to recent sales. This is fine, but there have not been many commercial sales in the last few years. One can modify this to examining the current competition on the market. What is the price per square foot of similar properties for sale? Another approach is the Cost Approach. What would it cost to replicate the subject property? This is especially important in valuing a GREEN buildings or property's that have has significant energy related improvements.

Valuation of investment properties or any commercial property today is not easy. Careful consideration must given to developing the current and future value.

Appreciation of Value

There are no guarantees that one's property will appreciate in value. However "based upon the numbers", and the CAP Rate formula we learned earlier we can project future value. Looking at our spread sheet, if we applied a conservative CAP Rate to the final year of the projected NOI, we would determine an anticipated value at that time.

Many investors will do this based upon how long they anticipate owning the building for, this is referred to as the **Holding Period**.

To understand this concept let's examine the values of the previous properties spreadsheet as calculated year by year with a conservative CAP Rate, eight percent (8%); using the CAP Rate formula to determine value.

$$\frac{NOI}{CAP\ Rate} = Value$$

Potential Future Value

Year	NOI	CAP Rate	Potential Value
1	$60,956	8%	$761,950
2	$73,664	8%	$920,800
3	$79,166	8%	$989,575
4	$87,384	8%	$1,092,300
5	$90,486	8%	$1,131,075

Keep in mind: Cap Rates are geographically and time sensitive – the change frequently and vary in different economic situations.

As we discussed today's reality may produce some up and down movement in the NOI forecasts and consequently the property's value may go down and then perhaps back up again. **These forecasts must be reality based.**

But to illustrate the next concept we will use these figures.

Internal Rate of Return (IRR)

The IRR serves as a basis of comparison for investors. It allows them to compare the performance of one investment to another. With real estate it takes into consideration the entire "life" of the transaction including:

- Initial Investment Amount
- Periodic Cash Flows
- Length of the Holding Period
- Reversion Proceeds (Disposition or Sale Proceeds).

These calculations can be done on a historical basis, reviewing the past performance of an investment, or will involve projecting the future incomes and the future sale price of the investment. This form of performance evaluation examines the time value of money.

Customers may also use IRR as a standard, expected or required return for their investments. Portfolio, REIT and institutional types of buyers commonly use the Internal Rate of Return.

The IRR is the discount rate at which the present value of future cash flows is exactly equal to the initial capital investment. Put another way the IRR is the rate earned by each dollar for each year that the dollar remains invested. **In practical terms the IRR reflects the effective rate of return each year while the property is/was owned**, taking into consideration the initial investment, all cash flows and ultimate sale proceeds.

Utilizing the NOI's as the annual cash flows and the cap rate values to determine the purchase price and sale price; at the end of the holding period we can calculate the IRR. This does require a specific type of calculator or program to do so. Below is the calculation for our Spread Sheet Example done on a Microsoft Excel program.

Internal Rate of Return

N	$			
0	-$761,960	Acquisition Price		
1	$60,956	NOI Cash Flow Yr. 1		
2	$73,664	NOI Cash Flow Yr. 2		
3	$79,166	NOI Cash Flow Yr. 3		
4	$87,384	NOI Cash Flow Yr. 4		
		NOI Cash Flow Yr. 5 +		
5	$1,221,641	Sales Proceeds	$90,286 +	$1,131,075
IRR	16.90%			

The first column (N) represents time. Time period "0" is the date of purchase reflecting the property cost. This is followed by the cash flows for years 1 through 5 reflected by each year NOI. In this calculation the purchase price is entered as a negative number. The cash flows are positive (in this case). The property is being held for five years, the calculation is time sensitive, therefore there are two financial events in year five, the cash flow and sale proceeds must be added together. Once this date is entered the IRR can be calculated. Rounding off, the resulting IRR is 17%, taking into consideration the annual cash flows and appreciation in value.

The annual average rate of return on this investment during the entire holding period of five years is 17% (rounded off).

If the property were being financed an IRR could also be determined. In this case the acquisition cost would be the Initial Investment or Down Payment. Each years cash flow would be the Cash Flow Before Taxes (CFBT) [NOI – ADS = CFBT]. The final year of ownership would reflect that years CFBT plus the Net Sales Proceeds after the mortgage was paid off. The calculation would be done as follows

Internal Rate of Return

N

0 **- Initial Investment (Down payment)**

1 **Cash Flow Before Taxes Yr. 1**

2 **CFBT Yr. 2**

3 **CFBT Yr. 3**

4 **CFBT Yr. 4**

5 **CFBT Yr. 5 + Net Sales Proceeds**

IRR **?**

Net Present Value (NPV)

Investors, generally institutional investors, use calculation methods similar to the IRR calculations to determine Net Present Value. Simply put **the NPV being what they can pay for a property to achieve a specific IRR return.** In this case the desired rate of return as well as the cash flows is known. Cap rate methodology is again be used to calculate a sale price at the end of the holding period. What will be calculated is the Acquisition Cost or the price one is willing to pay to achieve that desired rate of return. This would appear as below, utilizing the same data as the above example, but in this case seeking only a 15% return on investment.

Net Present Value

N	$		
0	?	Acquisition Price	
1	$60,956	NOI Cash Flow Yr. 1	
2	$73,664	NOI Cash Flow Yr. 2	
3	$79,166	NOI Cash Flow Yr. 3	
4	$87,384	NOI Cash Flow Yr. 4	
		NOI Cash Flow Yr. 5 +	
5	$1,221,641	Sales Proceeds	$90,286 + $1,131,075
IRR	15%		

Again, a specific type of calculator or program is required to do this calculation.

In this case to yield a 15% IRR over the five year holding period, **we calculated the most that could be paid for this property would be $818,092.**

To understand this better let's look at some "what if's". Based on the five year projections we showed a value in years two of $920,800 and Year 3 of $989,575 as a result of Upside Events (increases in rents). If the property were sold only on its current year NOI $60,956 at an 8% CAP Rate the sale price would be $761,960. But by showing the future values the seller established a $950,000 asking price, and someone paid $818,092.

The buyer would like to purchase the property for $761,960 realizing by using the IRR evaluation they would have a 16.90% return over five years. But by using NPV/IRR calculations to create a minimum acceptable IRR of 15% over five years they agreed to pay the $818,082 for the property

Part 4

Financing Your Purchase

Chapter 9: Commercial Property Loans

Buying a property with the help of "other people's money" or financing part of the purchase price always results in more profit for the owner. True or false?

Either answer may be correct. Basically the terms of the loan will dictate if the return on the investment will be greater than if the property were purchased for all cash.

In this chapter we will discuss financing the purchase of a property. Let us begin with some definitions of terms. "Other people's money" – Generally we look to banks to provide loans to purchase property. But you will need to provide a significant down payment; have you considered using the money in your IRA? Financing may be secured in several other ways; private lenders, the seller "holding paper" or providing a mortgage loan; syndication – getting a group of people together to contribute to the purchase. Corporations, Partnerships, Trusts may be formed to buy property or provide loans. "Crowdfunding" is the latest way for a group to invest in property.

Whenever one is going to enter into debt to purchase real estate it will be wise to discuss your plans and ways to finance with your attorney and accountant.

Very Important

Before "shopping" for real estate meet with your bank or financial consultant and determine exactly what you will need in the way of a down payment and closing costs. Know in advance how much of a loan you can get. In making an offer to purchase property the seller will want to know you have financing in place.

Financing Terms

Debt Service (Annual Debt Service) is the amount of money required to pay back to the lender each year of the loan term. This generally includes part of the principal of the loan and interest for that year. Typically loans are paid monthly, but for financial analysis purposes this figure is annualized (monthly payment multiplied by twelve months) and referred to as **Annual Debt Service**.

Loans made to purchase property are generally referred to as the "Mortgage". But in fact the "**Mortgage**" is a document that defines the property as collateral for the loan. A second document referred to as the **Note or Loan Agreement** defines the terms and details of the loan.

In some cases the seller of the property will desire to "hold the paper", provide the mortgage loan. They may provide the entire amount of the financing or, if the primary lender is not providing enough money, a secondary loan to the buyer.

There are many types of loans with different requirements for down payment amounts, the length of time the loan will be made for, and the interest rate to be charged. Loans are made for a specific period of time and are referred to as being **Amortized** over that period of time. Amortization tables show how much principal and how much interest is being paid with each payment. At the beginning of a loan the payment is mostly interest and at the end it is mostly principle. Generally as the term of the loan increases the monthly payment decreases. This may get to a point where all that is being paid is the interest. There are Interest Only loans and Negative-Amortization (where the monthly payment does not cover the monthly interest charge) but, we rarely see these in commercial purchases.

Balloon Mortgages

Very common in commercial financing are **Balloon Mortgages.** They are amortized over a long number of years, effectively reducing the monthly loan payment. However they are "Called in" meaning the loan ends and the outstanding balance of the loan is due after a shorter time period than the amortization schedule. This requires the pay off of the loan at that time, or refinancing. A balloon loan, for example, may be amortized over a 20 year term but it may be called in after 5 years.

The Balloon Mortgage Crises

The financial crisis of 2007-8 led to loss of values of commercial properties in the range of typically 25%-30%, some areas were harder hit and experienced loss of values of 40%-50%. As Balloon Mortgages became due during and after the devaluation, banks had new regulations and underwriting standards to comply with.

For example, a property was purchased in 2005. At that time the building was valued at $1,000,000. A loan was obtained for 75% of the value $750,000, with the buyer required to have a down payment of 25%, $250,000. The balloon loan was based on a 25 year amortization, but was due in 5 years. The bank basically implied that when the loan was called in 5 years; they would refinance it, but it might be at a slightly higher interest rate.

In 2010, the loan was due, and the outstanding amount of the loan was then $688,000. But values had dropped 25% and the property was then worth only $750,000. Underwriting standards have tightened and loans now require 30% down. Consequently the maximum amount the bank would loan on this building is $525,000.
($750,000 X 70% = $525,000)

The owner now owes $688,000; but the most the bank will refinance is $525,000. To refinance the loan the owner must come up with $163,000, or they default on the loan and the bank forecloses. This is an ugly reality of the times!

This truly presented a dilemma for many banks; complicated by the fact that most of these loans are not delinquent. Even thought the value of the building has declined the owner continues to make the loan payments in full and on time. The bank does not want to call in a performing loan and lose that relationship with their customer, but they have reserve and regulatory issues created by the loss of asset value. In many situations, as long as the loan is performing, we see the local banks taking what has become known as an "extend and pretend" position on the loan. As long as the payments are not in default the loan is temporally extended. The expectation being in the future the buildings value will again increase.

Key Lesson:

It is not always best to maximize loans on investment properties. Always consider you could lose tenants and cash flow or the market may "temporarily" decline values.

Self-Directed IRA's

Do you have money in your IRA accounts? It may be used to buy real estate. There are different types of IRA accounts some restrict ones investments to stocks, bonds and mutual funds. But a Self-Directed IRA is designed to hold alternative assets; primarily real estate. The first step is for you to speak to the company that services your IRA and find out if they permit a Self- Directed IRA.

When opening a Self-Directed IRA you do not have to close your current IRA. You can transfer as much or as little as you choose to your new account. If you do roll over the entire IRA to start a Self-Directed IRA you can still invest in all the traditional assets you wish. A self-directed IRA has all of the features of a traditional IRA with the added ability to hold alternative assets. Just like a traditional IRA, all appreciation and cash flow are tax deferred. Owning cash flow producing real estate in an IRA, offers a great stream of revenue which generally exceeds what you could achieve investing in annuities or stocks. Today many income properties are generating 7% - 8% or more in annual cash return, plus the long term appreciation in value. What a great way to build up your retirement account.

Another advantage of this type of IRA is that the IRA can borrow money. In other words you provide the down payment from your IRA to buy real estate and get a mortgage for the balance of the purchase price.

Self-directed does not mean you do everything yourself you need to work with a firm that does this, they will provide services as the custodian of your account.

Loan Underwriting

Debt Service Ratio (DSR)
Also known as the Debt Coverage Ratio (DCR)

Lenders want to be sure that an investment property has sufficient cash flow to support (pay back) the loan. They actually want the cash flow to be significantly greater than the amount of money required to pay annual debt service of the loan. This "cushion" tries to

absorb interruptions to the cash flow caused by vacancies or unexpected repairs. The lender establishes a minimum **Debt Service Ratio (DSR)** to regulate this. Historically most lenders required a DSR of 1.20 to 1.25. Today underwriters require 1.25 DSR or more.

The Net Operating Income (NOI) is the cash flow. The amount of money to be repaid to the lender in a year (principal and interest) is the Annual Debt Service (ADS).

Key Formula:

The NOI divided by the ADS
equals the Debt Service Ratio.

<u>Net Operating Income</u> = Debt Service Ratio or Debt Coverage Ratio
Annual Debt Service

As an example:

A property has income of $100,000, operating expenses of $40,000 and therefore has an NOI of $60,000. If the area CAP Rate were 8%; market value would be $750,000 (NOI divided by the CAP Rate equals Market Value).

Gross Operating Income	$100,000
Owner's Operating Expenses	- 40,000
Net Operating Income	$60,000

$$\frac{\$60,000 \ NOI}{.08 \ CAP \ Rate} = \$750,000 \ Market \ Value$$

A mortgage may be obtained requiring a 30% down payment, 7.5% interest and may be amortized over 20 years.

The $750,000 purchase would require a down payment of $225,000 and a mortgage loan of $525,000. Using a mortgage payment calculator the monthly payment on the loan is $4,229 (X 12 months) or Annual Debt Service of $50,752.

Dividing the Net Operating Income by the Annual Debt Service produces the Debt Service Ratio:

$$\frac{NOI}{ADS} = DSR$$

$$\frac{\$60,000 \; NOI}{\$50,752 \; ADS} = 1.18 \; DSR$$

In this case a Debt Service Ratio of 1.18. Most banks would have a problem making this loan, as it has too much risk. If the building losses a tenant they may not have sufficient cash flow to make the loan payments. Today most lenders want a Debt Service Ratio of 1.25 or higher to protect their loans.

As previously stated when the CAP Rate goes down the value or cost to buy the building goes up.

If our subject property sold at a 7% CAP, the purchase price would increase to $857,143. Using the same mortgage terms (30% down, 7.5% interest, 20 year term) the down payment would now be $257,143 with a $600,000 mortgage having Annual Debt Service of $58,002, barely covered by the cash flow of $60,000, with a Debt Service Ratio of 1.03.

$$\frac{\$60,000 \; NOI}{\$58,002 \; ADS} = 1.03 \; DSR$$

If our subject property sold at a 6% CAP the cash flow would be insufficient to cover the debt service.

Price $1,000,000, down $300,000, mortgage $700,000, Annual Debt Service $67,669. Not enough cash flow (NOI) $60,000 to pay the loan cost (ADS) of $67,669.

As we can see the debt service ratio must be carefully addressed when calculating how much of a down payment will be required to buy the property.

One solution to financing when the CAP Rates get low is for lenders to reduce their Debt Service Ratio requirements; which can be a challenge to their security of the loan. We may see some flexibility based upon low vacancy rates in an area and upon the strength of the tenants in the building. Prior to the economic crashes of 2008-2010 we saw some loans approved at 1.18 Debt Service Ratios, but it is now obvious that was not prudent.

A more likely solution will be in requiring higher down payments or reducing the purchase price to reduce the loan amount. Purchasing when CAP Rates are low may require 35% - 40% or more for the down payment.

Considering recent history and the current economic climate we can expect very little future flexibility on the part of lenders regarding their required debt service ratio for loans. **Today a solid 1.25 DSR is the norm.**

To calculate how much money may be available to repay a loan use the following formula:

$$\frac{NOI}{DSR} = \text{Total \$ Available for ADS}$$

Example:

$$\underline{\$50,000 \text{ NOI}} = \$40,000 \text{ Maximum ADS}$$
$$1.25 \text{ DSR}$$

In this case a proposed loan could require no more than $40,000 Annual Debt Service. Whatever amount you plug in as the NOI, divided by 1.25 resulting in the amount of money available for Annual Debt Service.

Loan to Value Ratio

Providing a mortgage loan is taking a risk on the part of the lender. They will qualify the borrower and generally seek participation in the risk in terms or requiring the borrower to make a significant down payment towards the purchase of the property. The underlying concern is in the event of a default on the loan; the lender will have to foreclose on the property and then may have to dispose of it at a discounted price below market value. If they only lend a portion of the market value their risk of loss in the event of foreclosure can be minimized.

Lenders establish a **Loan to Value (LTV) Ratio** based upon how much risk they are willing to take. The LTV is a percentage of Market Value. Market Value is determined by an Appraisal of the property.

If a bank had an LTV of 75%; they would consider loaning 75% of the Market (Appraised) Value of the property and expect the buyer to have a down payment of 25%.

Once again as a result of current market (fall, 2015) we see LTV's being a minimum of 30% and some requiring 35% to 40% as a down payment.

Loan to Value is calculated using the following formula:

Key Formula:

$$\underline{\textbf{Amount of Loan}} = \textbf{Loan to Value (LTV)}$$
Value of Property

For calculating loan to value the value of the property is the purchase price.

Example:

$$\underline{\textbf{Amount of loan \$650,000}} = \textbf{.065   65\% LTV}$$
Purchase Price \$1,000,000

Sources of Financing

Your local commercial bank and Credit Unions are the traditional sources of loans. When planning on investing in Real Estate you need to speak with them before you begin looking for property. They will guide you as to what types of loans they offer, what down payments they require, terms, interest rates and how much money they will loan you.

Prepare for the meeting by having a clear understanding of your investment goals. Know what type of property you wish to invest in. Explain your purpose and exit strategy. Is this purchase to house your business, or your business and more space to grow into, or your business and tenant income by design? If pure investment, how long do you plan to hold the building? I expect to fix the building up and sell it in a year. I expect to hold it for 10 years then sell. I want a 15 year straight mortgage; at the end of 15 year when I have paid off the loan I will sell the building. Or I intend to buy properties and hold them "forever".

If the purchase is for your business, have your business financials available. If a start up have a professional business plan developed.

Small Business Administration (SBA) Loans

Loans are available through this agency in a variety of programs. Loans are available to start a business or to buy a building to house that business in.

The SBA Express loan is designed for start-up businesses and has a loan limit of $350,000. The SAB 7 A is the most common loan, available to start up or expanding businesses with a $5 million dollar limit, but only $3.75 million is guaranteed by the SBA. The SBA 504 program is only for existing expanding business and loans up to $6 million.

There is a special program for Military Veterans to found or expand a business with loans up to $500,000.

When loan proceeds are used to purchase a building the building must be user occupied. However, if you are going to operate your business in the building you may be able to buy a larger building and rent the remainder out to other tenants. It will be required that you occupy at least 51% of the building.

All SBA programs will require personal guarantees by the borrowers. Also borrowers will need to provide 10% to 20% of the project funding themselves. The limits to the loan guarantee program are set annually by Congress.

Seller Financing "Holding Paper"

Sellers of properties, if they have little or no outstanding mortgage loan may desire to provide a mortgage loan to the buyer themselves. This creates additional income to them in the form of the interest they are charging. In many cases they will require a lower percentage of down payment than the banks.

In the event that the buyer cannot meet their obligation and defaults on the loan the original owner forecloses and gets the property back! Then they can sell it again.

In addition, there may be tax benefits as the capital gains taxes (discussed in a future chapter) will only be applied to the actual money received each year. This should be discussed with your tax advisor.

Interest is deductible

When leveraging a purchase by having a mortgage loan the buyer must provide the down payment and closing costs. The lender provides the balance of the purchase price but charges interest for this loan. The good news is that the interest charged on loans for buildings used in "your trade or business" are fully deductible in calculating the income tax on these properties. Under the 2018 tax laws, the mortgage interest deduction on your personal residence and one secondary residence is limited to $750,000 (More on this in a later chapter).

Crowdfunding

Crowdfunding is the practice of funding a purchase or project by raising many small amounts of money from large amounts of people, generally using the internet. This type of financing is regulated by the Security and Exchange Commission (SEC). There are many rules, limits and requirements; speak to an accountant or attorney for guidance.

The latest revisions in regulations were made in June, 2015, in an effort to make it easier for small businesses to raise capital. The new rules allow companies to raise up to $50 million under "Regulation A". However, any participant must be an "Accredited Investor"; defined as an individual with a net worth or joint net worth with a spouse that exceeds $1 million, excluding the value of their primary residence. Or an individual with annual income over $200,000 for the past two years, or joint income with a spouse over $300,000 for the past two years, with a reasonable expectation of the same income for the current year.

Another part of the law known as "Title III" will go into effect on January 29, 2016. This will allow "Unaccredited Investors" to participate in crowdfunding for ventures up to $1 million. Unaccredited Investors must having a net worth or current income of up to $100,000, they may invest the greater of $2,000 or 5% of their annual income or net worth in a 12 month period. With income or net worth over $100,000 one may invest up to 10% of either income or net worth.

Crowdfunding is regulated, there are rules and procedures to be followed; you must get professional assistance if you wish to raise capital in this manner.

Chapter 10: Cash on Cash Return
Also known as the Debt Equity Ratio

When a property has been financed the return on the investment is known as the **Cash on Cash Return (COC).** This is calculated based upon the monies left from the cash flow of the property after the annual debt service has been reconciled in relation to the initial investment.

The **Cash Flow Before Taxes (CFBT) a/k/a Before Tax Cash Flow (BTCF)** represents the monies left after the Annual Debt Service is subtracted from the Net Operating Income. The taxes being referred to in this context are the owner's income taxes. The **Initial Investment** is generally the down payment but may also include closing costs.

Key Formulas:

Net Operating Income
Less: Annual Debt Service
Cash Flow Before Taxes

$$\frac{\text{Cash Flow Before Taxes (CFBT)}}{\text{Initial Investment (II)}} = \text{Cash on Cash Return}$$

Example:

A property has income of $100,000, operating expenses of $40,000 and a NOI of $60,000. It is purchased for $700,000. The buyer finances the purchase with 30% down payment and obtains a mortgage loan based upon 7.5% interest amortized over 20 years. How are they doing on their investment?

Mortgage payments based upon financing $490,000 (70%) on the above terms would be $3,947 monthly, $47,369 Annual Debt Service. The Initial Investment (down payment of 30%) is $210,000.

Net Operating Income	$60,000
Less: Annual Debt Service	- $47,369
Cash Flow Before Taxes	$12,631

Cash Flow Before Taxes (CFBT) = Cash on Cash Return
Initial Investment (II)

$$\frac{\text{CFBT } \$12,631}{\text{II} \quad \$210,000} = .06 \quad \text{6\% Cash on Cash Return}$$

In this case leveraging (financing) the property yields the owner a 6% Cash on Cash return on their investment.

The terms of the loan affect the investors return on their investment. If we look at the same purchase, with a loan based upon 25 years and a 7% interest rate, note the different cash on cash return.

Mortgage payments based upon financing $490,000 (70%) on the above terms would be $3,463 monthly, $41,558 Annual Debt Service. The Initial Investment is $210,000.

Net Operating Income	$60,000
Less: Annual Debt Service	- $41,558
Cash Flow Before Taxes	$18,442

$$\frac{CFBT\ \ \$18,442}{\text{II}\ \ \ \ \$210,000} = .087 \qquad 9\% \text{ Cash on Cash Return}$$

In this case leveraging (financing) the property yields the owner a 9% Cash on Cash return on their investment.

As a final comparison what would the Return on Investment (ROI) be if the property were purchased all cash? Same property: $60,000 NOI, $700,000 Purchase Price.

$$\frac{\textbf{Net Operating Income (NOI)}}{\textbf{Market Value (Purchase Price)}} = \textbf{Return on Investment}$$

$$\frac{\$60,000}{\$700,000} = .0857 \qquad 8.6\% \text{ ROI}$$

Important Concept

Understand the impact of leveraging the purchase can create a higher or lower return on the investment than an all cash purchase, depending upon the terms of the loan.

Adding the concept of debt service to financial analysis, our cash flow analysis appears as follows:

Potential Rental Income

+ Additional Income from Tenants

- Vacancy and Credit Losses

= Effective Rental Income (sub-total)

+ Other Building Income

= Gross Operating Income

- Owners Operating Expenses

= Net Operating Income (NOI)

- Annual Debt Service (when financed)

= Cash Flow Before Taxes (CFBT)

The Cash- on-Cash Percentage Increases over Time

Another Example: A property was purchased for $2,000,000 with an initial investment (down payment) of $500,000. Currently the monthly cash flow, after all expenses and debt service has been paid is $15,000. What is the cash-on-cash return?

When doing financial calculations we must remember that all figures must be annualized.

$$\frac{\text{Cash Flow Before Taxes (CFBT)}}{\text{Initial Investment (II)}} = \text{Cash on Cash Return}$$

The monthly cash flow is $15,000 multiplied by 12 months is $180,000, annual cash flow before taxes.

$$\frac{\text{Cash Flow Before Taxes (CFBT) } \$180{,}000}{\text{Initial Investment (II) } \$500{,}000} = 36\% \text{ Cash on Cash Return}$$

Wow! A 36% return, almost sound too good to be true. Each year a property is owned we can expect the Cash-on-Cash percentage to increase. We expect the NOI of the building to increase every year, but the annual debt service remains constant causing the Cash Flow Before Taxes to also increase each year. The initial investment never changes, consequently the Cash-on-Cash percentage increase over time. In this example the property may have been owned 10 or more years to achieve this percentage.

This is a valid measurement of increased equity and value for the owner. But , a buyer would generally not be assuming the existing mortgage and would not focus on this measurement of return. Buyers look at the NIO of the property and calculate their purchase offers as if they were buying all cash (even though they will probably finance the purchase).

Part 5

Owning Investment Property

Chapter 11: Americans with Disabilities Act (ADA) and Fair Housing Law Requirements

As an investor one needs to be familiar with and comply with the ADA requirements.

Important
When buying a building, be sure it is ADA compliant. If it is not, negotiate with the owner to make it ADA compliant before you purchase it.

In most cases the requirements are not that expensive and may be offset by tax deductions and credits.

A disability is defined as a condition that limits one or more life activities, generally affecting mobility, vision or hearing. Approximately twenty percent of our Nations population has disabilities. Half of people over the age of 65 have a disability.

The Americans with Disabilities Act is one of the Federal Civil Rights Laws established to assist these individuals and prevent them from being discriminated against because of their disability. Discrimination can be in the form of intentional exclusion, physical barriers or failure to make reasonable modifications to existing facilities. There are many parts of this law regarding employers, communication, transportation but in this chapter we will focus on the laws pertaining to "public accommodations" (buildings open to the public) and building used in commerce – the commercial buildings we buy, sell or lease.

Today literally every commercial building must be accessible to those with disabilities. The ADA laws were expanded over the years requiring anyone who <u>owns, leases, lease to</u>, or operate facilities to make the building ADA compliant. Throughout the statutes examples are mentioned, such as restaurants, retail stores, hotels, movie theaters, private schools, convention centers, doctors' offices, homeless shelters, transportation depots, zoos, funeral homes, day care centers, and recreation facilities including sports stadiums and fitness clubs. Any building that is open to the public. Plus it covers businesses and nonprofit service providers that are public accommodations, privately operated entities offering certain types of courses and examinations and commercial facilities; all office and industrial buildings. Of note, both the landlord who owns the building and the tenant who owns or operates the place of public accommodation are subject to compliance.

What are we talking about doing? Basically, making buildings accessible to those in wheelchairs, installing ramps and handicapped bathrooms, creating accessible parking spaces and curb cuts, and other improvements to help those with disabilities. A discrimination suit could arise due to a failure to install an access ramp to a building presently only accessible by stairs. An example of discrimination, as illustrated on the ADA web site, is "a failure to remove architectural barriers…that are structural in nature, in existing facilities …where such removal is readily achievable". The key words are "readily achievable", the intent of the law is not to put one out of business. Some structural issues preventing compliance may be a legitimate excuse, for example, if we had adjacent buildings with stairs to enter, and no space to build a ramp. But the burden, if challenged, is on the property owner to justify why the building was not made ADA accessible.

In recent years "Recreational Access" was added to the ADA regulations. In particular this affects buildings that have pools, they must have one or more chair lifts depending upon size.

In many cases simple things; a person with arthritis could have difficulty turning a door knob. Changing that knob to a door handle is inexpensive, but could be very helpful. A bathroom may not be large enough to accommodate a wheelchair and there is a bearing wall making physical changes impossible, but wall rails or grab bars to assist some people could be installed. Fire alarms need to be updated in building to include strobe lights, for the hard of hearing and sounds for those with vision impairments.

Doing common sense things to help those with disabilities is the intent of the act., if a blind person comes into a restaurant, the waiter or waitress need to read them the menu (you don't need braille menus).

Service animals are required to be permitted in all places open to the public. This is federal law, even if the local building department prohibits animals in a building. Service animals are defined as dogs and miniature horses only; that are specifically trained to assist the person with their handicap. Emotional support animals are not service animals.

Another concern is do I have to put in an elevator? If the building is less than three stories or has less than 3,000 square feet per story an elevator is not required, unless the building is a shopping center, a shopping mall, or the professional office of a health care provider.

There is another common misconception that older buildings are exempt from ADA compliance. This is not true; there is no grandfathering regarding ADA laws.

This is federal law, enforced by the U. S. Department of Justice. There can be severe penalties for non-compliance or discrimination. A first offense fine could be as much as $50,000; subsequent fines up to $100,000.

On the positive side, efforts to comply can result in tax credits of up to $5,000 per year, based on 50% of the cost up to $10,000. Plus tax deductions of up to $15,000 may be taken every per year. All ADA improvements do not need to be done at once. If some improvements are made every year it shows a pattern of compliance. In most cases the improvements costs are offset by the tax deductions and credits available.

We mentioned earlier 20% of the population has a disability in one form or another and half of folks over 65 have problems. Make your buildings accessible to everyone. Of note, especially if your property is office or retail, these potential customers have over $178 Billion dollars to spend as disposable income each year.

Commercial property owners need to be familiar with the ADA statutes. There is a web site www.ADA.gov that is very helpful and includes some excellent video tutorials.

Fair Housing Laws

The Fair Housing Act of 1968 prohibits discrimination in the sale, rental or advertising of housing. The act prohibits housing discrimination on the basis of race, color, religion, sex, disability, familial status, and national origin. This is federal law administered by the Department of Housing and Urban Development (HUD), usually enforced on a State level.

Obviously these laws will apply to any residential properties, but also include multi-family and mixed use buildings. We will look at a few of the statutes that apply to properties you might invest in.

The law specifically requires: **that new multifamily housing with four or more units be designed and built to allow access for persons with disabilities.** This includes accessible common use areas, doors that are wide enough for wheelchairs, kitchens and bathrooms that allow a person using a wheelchair to maneuver, and other adaptable features within the units.

There is a practical issue here; if you build 200 units do all have to be ADA accessible. Probably not, the intent is to provide adequate handicap accommodations for the project. More than likely a meeting with the local building department, the developer, a

HUD representative, and other concerned parties will occur to discuss demographics and local statistics on age and disabled persons in the area and come up with a reasonable percentage of the units to be made ADA accessible, perhaps 20%-25%. This will be reviewed on a case by case basis.

The Fair Housing Act requires owners of housing facilities to make "reasonable accommodations", exceptions in their policies and operations to afford people with disabilities equal housing opportunities. For example, a landlord with a "no pets" policy may be required to grant an exception to this rule and allow an individual who is blind to keep a service animal in the residence.

I had a student in one of my classes, who owned a ten unit apartment house, tell this story. They had a blind person with a Seeing Eye Dog apply to rent one of their apartments. They were about to make an exception to their "no pets" policy when one of their existing tenants found out about the potential new renter. They came to the owner and voiced their concern, saying that the reason they rented in this building was because of the "no pets" policy. Explaining, they have terrible allergies to animals. Consequently the owner denied renting to the blind person. If challenged, this would be a legitimate excuse for not complying with the ADA Act.

The Fair Housing guidelines now includes giving "reasonable accommodations" to people with Emotional Support Animals (ESA), an animal that provides the owner with companionship or comfort. The need for an Emotional Support Animal must be documented with a certification letter from a Doctor or Mental Health Provider.

The Fair Housing Act also requires landlords to allow tenants with disabilities to make reasonable access-related modifications to their private living space, as well as to common use spaces. But the landlord is not required to pay for the changes. Once again, it is the intent of the law to help people with disabilities.

HUD investigates and enforces complaints of housing discrimination and violations of the Fair Housing Laws; penalties for violations start with $10,000 fines.

Chapter 12: Improving your Building and "Green" Concepts

In order to acquire new tenants and retain existing tenants your building and grounds must be well maintained, kept clean and regularly updated. Establish a budget for these necessities.

But also consider the unexpected; create a contingency emergency repair fund. What if the roofs starts to leak or worse collapses from the weight of snow, or if your air conditioning or heating system fails and must be replaced; money need to be set aside for these possibilities. This "Repair and Maintenance Fund" or "Replacement Reserves" (It does not matter what you call it) amount of money, should be based on the age and condition of your building. A good "rule of thumb" in determining the amount is to use 5%-10% of your Gross Income.

Very Important
Create a contingency emergency repair fund.

We keep hearing the term "Green", what is it? With people the term Green really represents a state of mind; a consciousness towards ecology and energy efficiency. Simple initiatives like recycling, using efficient light bulbs, turning off lights, water constricting devises in bathrooms, all help our environment. But the big picture is the necessity to reduce the Carbon Emissions or ''Greenhouse Gasses'' from our buildings, which have caused the drastic climate changes we are all experiencing.

For the past 100 + years, as the different countries on earth developed their resources, greenhouse gases were produced as a by-product. The buildup of these carbon emissions has caused erosion of the ozone layer that protects our planet from the heat of the sun. This is causing the climate changes we now see every day, severe storms, excessive temperatures in the summer, droughts, the Polar Vortex affect in winter.

From a practical view green is thought of as improving the energy efficiency and air quality of a building, from an environmental point of view it means reducing the carbon emissions of that building. In the United States we have 4.8 million commercial buildings and 350,000 industrial buildings which consume 40% of energy use and 72% of electricity and produce 39% of all carbon emissions.

For many people, especially in the Northeast, Hurricane Sandy was a great awakening. Part of the climate changes is the melting of the north and south poles which increases the level of the oceans. As a result of this, the hurricane pushed the ocean over the New York City sea walls and flooded out the city and many other parts of the tri-state region.

In October 2015 Hurricane Joaquin pounded the Mid-Atlantic States with 27 inches of rain in two days, causing Billions of dollars in damage. Most damage was to roads and bridges which must be replaced.

Our Government and Governments all over the world are now very focused on climate changes because all of these natural disasters require billions of dollars in rescue, recovery and infrastructure repair. **Many cities in the U.S. are now requiring new construction and alterations of buildings be constructed in a "green" fashion with third party certifications.**

This is global problem which must be solved. In the December, 2015 Paris Environmental Agreement 160 countries pledged to reduce their carbon emissions by developing more renewable energy using, wind, solar, hydro and geothermal sources.

With buildings it means a focus on construction or improvements that create energy efficiency and promote environmental sustainability.

Key Concept

Sustainability is the concept of using resources wisely to satisfy today's requirements without compromising the ability of future generations to do the same.

In buildings the primary areas we can improve upon are energy consumption, indoor air quality, efficiency in heating and cooling systems and water conservation.

Today's technology has given us many ways to improve our buildings energy use and reduce our carbon emissions. Solar power is now affordable and installing it on a commercial roof may produce all the electricity that the building needs. Heating and air conditioning systems are now more efficient and designed to use less power, add

Programmable thermostats to your building to further reduce energy use. Geothermal heating and cooling can virtually eliminate fuel expense. (This is based on the constant temperature at certain depths within the earth. It is still expensive, but practical for new construction.)

Recycle the condensation from your air conditioning system to water the landscaping or other uses. Simple things like installing inexpensive aerators on the plumbing facilities can conserve water and lower costs. Window and door seals periodically deteriorate; attention and maintenance here can be a big savings. Lighting systems today can reduce electric cost by 30% or more, they also give off less heat reducing cooling costs and the bulbs last much longer.

Installing these features in your building will reduce your operating expenses.

Key Concept

Besides helping the environment, when the operating costs of a building can be reduced, this saves the owner money. If any operating expenses that are paid by or passed through to tenants are reduced, they save money, making the building more attractive to tenants.

Going Green – figuring the payback

One of the biggest challenges building owners have, when considering to "green" their building is how and when I get a payback. Simply put, to make their building more energy efficient, and from a sustainable point of view, reduce the buildings carbon emissions, will cost a lot of money. What is the return on the investment?

For most items the cost of the improvements can be recapped through depreciation or expensing. Under the tax benefits passes in December 2015 most interior improvements can be depreciated over 15 years (now permanent) or with 50% Bonus Depreciation (through 2017, then reduced and phase out). Expending (Section 179) has now been restored to up to a $500,000 deduction and has been made permanent. Plus, it now includes air conditioning and heating units. From a tax point of view these deductions are great recovery. **See Chapter 13 "Depreciation and Cost Recovery" for 2018 additional tax changes.**

But from a cash flow point of view where is my return on investment? The capital outlay for energy improvements will result in how much in savings? Based on that how long will the payback period be?

For example, if I spend $10,000 to put all new energy efficient lighting in my building how long till I recover that expense. Assume the resulting savings in electric costs will be $3,000 per year.

This can be easily calculated using the following "Simple Payback" formula:

$$\frac{\text{Cost}}{\text{Annual Savings}} = \text{Pay Back in Years}$$

$$\frac{\text{Cost}}{\text{Annual Savings}} \quad \frac{\$10,000}{\$3,000} = 3.3 \text{ years for payback}$$

After 3.3 years we would have recovered the cash outlay. This same formula/concept applies to considering any improvement to your building.

In addition to using less wattage and reducing the kilowatts used there are other benefits too. The new technology of light bulbs last much longer, see the below chart comparing energy uses to produce 60,000 hours of light:

60,000 Hours of Light	Lifespan Hours	Watts	Kilowatts Used
Incandescent Bulbs	1,500	60	3,600
Compact Fluorescent Lamps (CFL)	10,000	14	840
Light Emitting Diodes (LED)	60,000	6	360

Also, the newer energy efficient light bulbs virtually produce no heat as compared to the old incandescent bulbs, reducing the cost to cool the building.

In figuring the "pay back", the bigger picture needs to look at when improving the entire building. If the landlord's leases are Gross of Full Service; the landlord collects a high amount of rent from the tenants and pays the operating expenses of the building from the money collected. If the landlord improves the energy efficiency of the building they will reduce their operating costs and have more profit; a higher Net Operating Income. But in this case there is no benefit to the tenant.

If the landlord's leases are "Triple Net (NNN)" the tenant is charged lower rent but the tenant is responsible to pay all the operating costs. When the landlord improves the energy efficiency of the building the tenants operating expenses are reduced. Other types of leases, Modified Gross or Net, may also reduce the tenants operating cost.

These reductions benefit the tenant, not the landlord. So, in this situation how does the landlord recoup the monies paid for the building improvements?

The dilemma of having the landlord recoup their capital outlay for improvements while giving the benefit of the expense reductions to the tenant was solved by then Mayor Bloomberg's Office of Long Term Planning and Sustainability. The answer has become known as the "split incentive" scenario and was part of the first Green Lease in NYC at the LEED Gold Certified, 7 World Trade Center. (LEED will be discussed later)

Split Incentive Scenario
The Landlord pays for the capital improvements but does not benefit from any reductions in the operating expenses because the tenant pays the operating expenses per the lease. The landlord wishes to recover the costs of those improvements from the tenant(s) based on a "Simple Payback", not through "useful life" tax depreciation.

The lease language would read: "Landlord may include in the operating expenses (to be paid by the tenant) the aggregate costs of such capital improvements, not to exceed

110

80% of the projected annual savings. The aggregate costs of such capital improvements will be fully amortized over 125% of the simple payback period."

For example: the Capital Improvements cost $2,000,000; when completed the projected annual savings will be $500,000. The "Simple Payback" formula establishes a 4 year or 48 month payback.

$$\frac{\text{Cost}}{\text{Annual Savings}} \quad \frac{\$2,000,000}{\$500,000} \quad = \quad 4 \text{ years or 48 months for payback}$$

According to the above lease language, the landlord will add to the tenants operating expenses 80% or the projected saving $500,000 X .80 (80%) = $400,000 as a repayment to the landlord for the capital improvements expense annually, for 125% of the "Simple Payback" period. Four years or 48 months X 1.25 (125%) = 60 months or five years.

The buildings operating expenses have been reduced by $500,000 as a result of the landlord's improvements. During the first five years of the lease the tenant gets the benefit of the operating expense reduction, but must pay the landlord $400,000 annually as a contribution to the construction costs. The tenant has a net reduction of $100,000 in operating expenses annually. After the initial five year period the landlord has recouped the full $2,000,000 they sent on capital improvements and the tenant now gets the full benefit of the $500,000 reduction in the buildings operating expenses.

There are other considerations too. If the landlord reduces the operating expenses of the building and passes the savings on to the tenants, the building may become more desirable or the landlord could charge more rent.

As a result of the new energy efficiency in the building the carbon footprint of the building will be reduced. Carbon emissions can now be measured; a reduction will increase the value of buildings.

In evaluating the investment opportunity consider buying a Green building or rehabbing a building to be Green. Whether you reduce your operating expenses or pass thru the savings to the tenants, a "Simple Payback" is possible. From a marketing point of view "greening" will help you secure new tenants or sell the building at a higher price.

The Beginning of Rating Systems

Energy Star was the first rating system, started in 1992 by the Environmental Protection Agency (EPA) and the Department of Energy (DEP). Initially, it rated products that use 20%-30% less energy.

Then they expanded to rating homes and commercial buildings. The EPA conducts periodic surveys known as CBECS, the Commercial Buildings Energy Consumption Survey. The statistics are used to create models of best and worst system performance. Using a performance scale of 1-100; a building that is more energy efficient than similar buildings, with a rating of 50 is considered an Energy Star Rated Building When achieving 75 on the comparison scale the building is awarded the Energy Star Label.

Owners complete an extensive application of energy consumption and improvements which must be verified by a third party for certification. As of 2014 there were over 25,000 commercial buildings and plants Energy Star rated in the United States. The EPA also presents awards for Energy Star Leaders – Top Energy Performance and Energy Star Partners – Recognizes outstanding contributions to reduce greenhouse gas emissions through energy efficiency.

One of the 2014 Energy Start Partners was Kohl's Department Stores. The award was based on their energy efficient improvements and the reduction of carbon emissions from their buildings. Out of 1,158 Stores, 910 are Energy Star Certified in addition 453 are LEED Certified Buildings. Plus 160 of their stores have solar paneled roof, that create enough power to supply the store and sell the excess electricity to the local grid. In total, including their warehouse facilities they have 35,671,412 SF of energy efficient and environmentally friendly space.

Another rating system was developed in Canada and is also used in some buildings in boarding US States, called "Green Globes". It is a point system based on the opportunity of earn up to 1,000 points base on energy efficiency of improvements in your building. One to five Green Globes are awarded; it is also owner applied and third party verified.

In 1998 the US Green Building Council (USGBC) introduced Leadership in Energy and Environmental Design (LEED). This is a rating system on new construction or improvements to an existing building. What LEED effectively did was answer the question, "How do I make my building green". LEED provides building owners and operators a concise framework for identifying and implementing practical and measurable green building design, construction, operations and maintenance solutions. It address all facets of the building from site selection (for a new building), lighting and water efficiencies, indoor air quality, construction materials and how to minimizing carbon emissions.

LEED has given us the foundation to improve our buildings and LEED Certification is now recognized as a prestigious accomplishment of the building's owners. Up to 100 points are earned in six categories: materials used, sustainability sites, energy conservation, water efficiency, environmental quality and innovation and design process. Based upon earning the required number of points buildings are rated LEED Certified (40 points), LEED Silver (50 points), LEED Gold (60 points or LEED Platinum (80 points). Certifications are available for new construction, major renovations, existing operations, commercial interiors (fit out by tenants) and homes.

Each point represents a process of saving energy or helping the environment. There are as of October, 2015 over 53,900 LEED certified building in the United States, 83,400 buildings worldwide; representing 13.8 billion square feet. It is projected by the USGBC that by 2016 half of the new construction in the US will be green.

Owners can improve their buildings without getting them LEED certified and many do. But the question arises, perhaps in a potential tenants mind, "…the owner says his building is green but what have they actually done?" By having a building LEED certified an owner has proof that the building is green. Certification is done by the USGBC's Green Building Certification Institute, an independent third party verification of the work done on the building. The LEED certification also requires the building be maintained at these standards and go through a recertification process within five years or lose the rating.

Building with "Green" construction materials today costs about the same as conventional building; the design aspect however may be a bit more. Also to have the property certified by the rating systems adds to the costs.

The real benefit of following the LEED guidelines shows up in the reduction of the buildings operating expenses; using less water and electricity, reducing heat and air conditioning cost. When we reduce operating costs we increase the net operating income (NOI) of the building; as the NOI increases so does the value of the property.

In some leases the operating costs are "passed through" for the tenants to pay. If the owner improves the buildings efficiency these savings are then benefits to the tenants, making this building more competitive in attracting and retaining tenants.

Today we have the technology to measure the results of these improvements. We can monitor how much electricity and water is consumed in a building, the indoor air quality and the carbon emissions produced. In NYC a law went into effect last year requiring buildings of 50,000 SF or more to "benchmark" (record) these statistics. A future measurement will show if the building is improving or getting worse. With the serious focus on reducing carbon emissions, the buildings that do so will be considered more valuable.

There is also another benefit of constructing or renovating using LEED standards, we have a happier and healthier work environment. Better indoor air quality, better lighting, more windows or interior glass walls allowing more workers to "see the sun" create a better atmosphere to work in. We now have statistics that employees working in green buildings take fewer sick days and are more productive. Good news for the employer who also sees better retention of their employees.

The Future of Green

Landlord and tenants today are creating "Green Leases", working together to promote green principals within the workplace and work space. Our Government is also becoming more proactive with concerns for climate changes and carbon emissions. A recent bill was proposed to energy rate homes and buildings. Many municipalities are now requiring new buildings and rehabs to be LEED certified or providing Tax incentives for Green construction.

Some legislators are now talking about imposing a "Carbon Tax" on the buildings or plants that do not stabilize and reduce their carbon emissions

GREEN is the future out of necessity. Actions must be taken to safeguard our world; energy saving technology is here now and affordable. Buildings can be designed or improved to be "smarter", more energy efficient, improving indoor air quality, conserving water and reducing operating costs, while helping the environment.

Non-green building in the future will become obsolete. Investors need to focus on the benefits of going GREEN.

Chapter 13: Depreciation or Cost Recovery

In reality "depreciation" represents the wear and tear on a building over time. As buildings age certain systems within it become old; obsolescence begins. An older building may have an electric system with fuses; the more modern building uses circuit breakers. Roofs, heating systems, plumbing are all subject to such wear and tear. The exterior and interior structure of the building, the grounds, parking lots all require upgrading and maintenance to counter natural deterioration.

The IRS recognizes this and has established rules to allow the owner to depreciate their building for estimated wear, tear and obsolescence.

- Depreciation does not apply to your Personal Residence; but **depreciation is required on all investment property**
- Land does not depreciate
- Residential type buildings are depreciated over 27 ½ years
- Commercial type buildings are depreciated over 39 years
- Capital Improvements must also be depreciated

Land does not depreciate. When a property is purchased the value of the land and the value of the building must be segregated. Generally with commercial property purchases a formal appraisal is conducted and it will include this analysis.

Residential type buildings include single family homes (not your personal residence), duplexes, three or four family structures and larger apartment houses.

Typical Commercial type buildings are offices, retail, industrial, or combinations thereof.

Settlement fees and closing costs may be included in determining the cost basis of the property. Examples are: abstract and title fees, legal fees, title searches, recording fees, surveys, title insurance, transfer taxes and charges for installing utility services.

Also any amounts the seller owes that the buyer agrees to pay may be included in the cost basis. These categories would include: back taxes, interest, recording fees, charges for improvements or repairs and sales commissions.

If you buy a property and assume an existing mortgage your cost basis will include the amount paid plus the amount of the outstanding mortgage.

Buildings are depreciated using the straight-line depreciation method. Meaning the value (cost basis) is divided by 27.5 (residential type) or 39 (commercial type) to determine an equal amount of depreciation allowance each year.

Example of Depreciation:

Small Office Building
Depreciation schedule 39 years

Purchase Price	$495,000
Title Search & Insurance	1,800
Survey	2,200
Legal Fees	1,000
Acquisition Cost	$500,000
Less Land Value	- 110,000
Cost Basis	$390,000
Recovery Period	÷ 39 years
Depreciable Allowance	$ 10,000

Each year that the building is owned (up to 39 years) the owner may deduct $10,000 from the taxable income of the property for depreciation.

Mixed use buildings, containing both residential and commercial units may have two depreciation schedules; an accountant needs to be consulted to establish the depreciation schedules for these types of buildings. The general rule however, is that a building must be 80% residential to qualify for the accelerated 27.5 year depreciation schedule.

Leasehold Improvements a/k/a Tenant Improvements (TI)

Prior to 2004 the costs of commercial leasehold improvements were depreciated over 39 years. In 2004 the depreciation schedule for certain leasehold improvements was reduced to 15 years. This had been set to expire annually but was extended on a yearly basis, until the end of 2014. More on this shortly.

In 2008 the "leasehold improvement category" was expanded to include restaurant buildings and improvements, and retail improvements. This reduced cost recovery time schedule for these items actually expired at the end of 2009; however in the Reauthorization and Job Creation act of 2010 the special 15 year cost recovery period for certain leasehold improvements, restaurant buildings and improvements and retail improvements was extended by two years; this was retroactive to January 1, 2010.

Congress has been in the habit of reviewing these tax breaks in December of each year and reauthorizing them retroactive to January 1 of that year; known as "Tax Extender Legislation". Consequently the 15 year recovery period had been extended each year since 2010, but it again expired on December 31, 2014. See the following.

2015 Extender Bill Passed

Each December the U.S. Congress passes a series of bills known as the Omnibus Appropriations Bills, which authorize the funding of the government for the following year. They include a group of items referred to as "extenders"; in this category they look at tax breaks that expired at the end of the previous year, Deciding if they wish to extend them and making the extension retroactive to January first of the current year. Typically they are only extended to December 31 of the current year, leaving everyone in limbo as the upcoming year's status.

Confuse yet? For example, on December 31, 2013 the 15 year depreciation recovery for leasehold improvements expired. During the year 2014 leasehold improvement depreciation reverted back to 27.5 or 39 years depending on the type of property. However, in December of 2014, as part of that year's extender bill, 15 year depreciation recovery for leasehold improvements was extended to December 31, 2014, retroactive to January 1, 2014.

Things were very different in the 2015 tax extender bills, some tax benefits were made permanent and some were extended for multiple years. Then in 2018 things changed again.

2018 Commercial Real Estate Tax Benefits Changes

Effective 2018, many of the tax laws pertaining to real estate changed.

Depreciation

The new bill retains that depreciation of commercial buildings will be over 39 years and depreciation of residential buildings will be over 27.5 years. To qualify for the accelerated residential depreciation the building must be 80% or more residential use (by square footage).

15 year Cost Recovery remains available for Qualified Improvement Property. However the definition of Qualified Improvement Property used in Depreciation and Section 179 Expensing has changed.

Qualified Property has previously included and will generally continue to apply to:

- Personal property used in trade or business
- Off the shelf computer software
- Qualified Real Property
    Leasehold Improvements (interior nonresidential)
    Qualified Restaurant Property (~~purchase of building*~~ or improvements)
    Qualified retail improvements (only in areas open to the public)
- Passenger Automobiles (other limits apply)

*The major change here is: Restaurant <u>building</u> property placed in service after Dec. 31, 2017, no longer meets the definition of qualified improvement property, and is now depreciable as nonresidential real property over 39 years.

For property placed in service after Dec. 31, 2017, the separate definitions of qualified leasehold improvement, qualified restaurant, and qualified retail improvement property are eliminated, a general 15-year recovery period and straight-line depreciation are provided for qualified improvement property.

Qualified improvement property is now defined as "any improvement to an interior portion of a building that is nonresidential real property if such improvement is placed in service after the date such building was first placed in service".

However qualified improvement property does not include any improvement for which the expenditure is attributable to the enlargement of the building, any elevator or escalator, or the internal structural framework of the building.

Eligible property used in trade or business are interior improvements to nonresidential buildings. Previously the rule required that items purchase must be new; it now allows for purchase of new or used items.

Bonus Depreciation

Effective September 28, 2017, 100% of the cost of eligible property may be depreciated in the year of purchase; this will end December 31, 2022. Thereafter the Bonus Depreciation will phase down: 80% in 2023, 60% in 2024, 40% in 2025, 20% in 2026, then 0% in 2027.

Section 179 Expensing

A taxpayer may elect under Section 179 to deduct (or "expense") the cost of qualified property, rather than to recover such costs through depreciation deductions. The limit has been raised to $1,000,000 with a phase out threshold of $2,500,000, for property placed in service after December 31, 2017.

Added coverages for qualified property eligible for section 179 expensing now include:

- Property to furnish lodgings
- For nonresidential real estate roofs, heating, ventilation, air conditioning, fire protection and alarms and security systems

Eligible amount for expensing may not exceed taxable income for the year, but may be carried forward to successive years.

Investment Tax Credit ("ITC")

The ITC for solar will now continue at 30 percent levels for both commercial and residential systems through 2019, then reduced to 26% in 2020, 22% in 2021 and will settle at 10 percent in 2022.

Always check with your tax advisor for the current status and treatment of any Capital Improvements.

Cost Segregation

There are ways to break down the cost components in construction and with certain improvements and depreciate these costs over different time periods. This is known as

Cost Segregation. This will provide shorter depreciation time periods for personal property (5 years or 7 years) and for land improvements (15 years) resulting in higher depreciation in the early years of owning the building. Again check with your tax advisor to determine if this can be beneficial to you.

Establishing depreciation schedules should be done with the advice of an accountant or tax advisor.

Tax Shelter

Depreciation which is also known as Cost Recovery is considered the best tax shelter as it may create "paper losses" which can offset taxable gains.

Important Concept:

The taxable gain on ones property is determined by subtracting from the income four categories of expenses: operating expenses, real estate taxes, mortgage interest and depreciation. The gain or profit is then taxed based on the taxpayer's marginal tax rate.

For example:

An apartment building has $65,000 in rental income, operating expenses of $13,000, real estate taxes of $12,000.

There is a mortgage costing $32,000 a year of which $24,000 is interest. Being residential type property the depreciation schedule is based on 27.5 years and the annual depreciation allowance is $20,000.

See below the actual cash flow of the property versus the taxable consequences when depreciation and other deductions are considered.

From a Cash Flow viewpoint:

Income	$65,000	
Less Expenses:		
Operating Costs	- 13,000	
R.E. Taxes	- 12,000	
NOI	$40,000	(Net Operating Income)
Less ADS	- 32,000	(Annual Debt Service)
Cash Flow	$8,000	

From a Taxable Gain viewpoint:

Income	$65,000
Less Deductions:	
Operating Costs	- 13,000
R.E. Taxes	- 12,000
Mortgage Interest	- 24,000
Depreciation	- 20,000
Total Deductions	$69,000
"Paper Loss"	- $4,000

As a result of depreciation this property shows a loss for this year and consequently there is no taxable gain, no income taxes due. But in reality the owner had a profit of $8,000. In most cases depreciation will not cause an overall loss as in this example, but it will reduce the taxable gain.

Chapter 14: Taxes on Your Property

Each year you will have to pay taxes on the real estate you own. Depending which State you reside in this may be in the form of Real Property Taxes or Personal Property Taxes; in addition there may be School Taxes and Local Government Taxes. The owner of the property, individual or business entity (Corporation, partnership, trust, etc.) may also have to pay annual Income Taxes on the property.

When you finally sell your investment you will be subject to capital gains taxes. On investment property the capital gains taxes may be deferred by using a 1031 tax deferred exchange. This chapter will show how Income Taxes are calculated, in Chapters 18 and 19 we will explore Capital Gains Taxes and 1031 Exchanges.

2018 Tax Changes

The marginal tax brackets as of January 1, 2018 will be: 10%, 12%, 22%, 24%, 33%, 35% and 37%. Each year they will be modified for inflation.

Below are the tax brackets as of 2016:

Tax Bracket	Single Taxpayer	Married Taxpayer
10%	0 - $9,525	0 - $19,050
12%	$9,525 - $38,700	$19,050 - $77,400
22%	$38,700 - $82,500	$77,400 - $165,000
24%	$82,500 - $157,500	$165,000 - $315,000
32%	$157,500- $200,000	$315,000 - $400,000
35%	$200,000 - $500,000	$400,000 - $600,000
37%	Over $500,000	Over $600,000

Net Investment Income Tax also being called the "Medicare Surcharge" Tax

The Medicare Surcharge Tax remains in effect. This 3.8% tax is due on individuals, estates and trusts if the taxpayer has Net Investment Income and adjusted gross income (AGI) of $200,000 as an individual or $250,000 filing as married. The tax is based on the excess AGI or the Net Investment Income, whatever the lesser amount is. These figures will not be indexed for inflation.

Example 1

- John has a job that pays him $85,000 a year.
- Plus he owns a small apartment building that has gross rents of $130,000 this year.
- He also has expenses relating to the apartment income.

Tax Analysis

AGI from Job	$85,000
Gross rents from apartment building	$130,000
Less expenses*	$110,000
Net Investment Income	$20,000
New AGI	$105,000

Since the AGI is under $200,000 (single) no additional tax is due.

*Expenses include depreciation and mortgage interest.

Example 2

- John and Mary are married, both work and have combined income of $285,000.
- They own a small apartment building that has gross rents of $130,000 this year.
- They also have expenses relating to the apartment income.
- They file their taxes jointly.

Tax Analysis

AGI from their jobs	$285,000
Gross rents from apartment building	$130,000
Less expenses	$110,000
Net Investment Income	$20,000
New AGI	$305,000
Excess AGI over $250,000 (married)	$55,000

The tax is based on the lesser of the AGI or Net Investment Income.

Net Investment Income $20,000 X .038 (3.8%) = $760

John and Mary will have to pay an additional tax of $760 Medicare Surcharge.

Itemized Deduction Limits and the "Pease" provision phase out have been repealed starting with the 2018 tax year.

As of January 1, 2018 there are no individual deduction limits.

Alternative Minimum Tax (AMT)

Threshold limits have been raised to $70, 300 for singles and $109,400 for married filing jointly for 2018 tax filings. The phase out has also be increased to $500,000 single and $1,000,000 married filing jointly.

The Corporate Alternative Minimum Tax has been repealed starting in 2018.

Mortgage Interest Deduction

This deduction as of January 1, 2018 is limited to mortgage interest paid up to a $750,000 acquisition loan.

The deduction may be applied to personal residence and one secondary residence.

Home Equity Interest is no longer deductible.

Deductions for Taxes Paid

Deductions for your personal State and Local property taxes and sales taxes "SALT" paid are now limited to a total deduction of $10,000. There is no limit for taxes paid for Trade or Business properties.

Corporate Taxes

The Corporate tax rate has been reduced to 21%.

Small Business - Qualified Business Income

The new tax law, effective January 1, 2018 provides Sole Practitioners (Independent Contractors), LLC's, Partnerships and S Corporations a 20% deduction of business income. Excluded are "Personal Service Businesses". Defined as "Any business where the main asset of the business is the reputation or skill of one or more of its employees or owners."

Real estate agents and brokers are in this category. However, the National Association of Realtors secured an exception for single owners with taxable income under $157,500 and for couples filing jointly with taxable income under $315,000. The deduction is phased out for income above this and eliminated on single income over $207,000 and couples filing jointly income over $415,000. This exception applies to anyone in the "Personal Service Business" category.

Entertainment Expenses

Entertainment of clients expenses (50% of costs) were deductible for 2017; but are <u>no longer deductible in 2018.</u>

The 50% deduction for food and drink associated with business or work travel still remains deductible.

Tax Preparation Fees

Tax preparation fees paid in 2017 are deductible, but <u>in 2018 they will no longer be a deduction.</u>

Cash Flow After Taxes (CFAT)

The annual income you receive from your investment property is subject to income tax. You may deduct from that gross income the operating expenses of the property, real estate property taxes, interest on mortgage loans and depreciation, subject to the aforementioned limitations as of 2018. The remaining net income is taxed at the taxpayer's marginal tax rate. What remains after payment of income taxes is the After Tax Cash Flow (ATCF) or as it is also called the Cash Flow After Taxes (CFAT). The Cash Flow Before Taxes (CFBT) truly reflects "what is left" annually from the cash flow of one's investment property. From this Income Taxes must be paid.

However an additional adjustment "to the numbers" is required before the tax calculations are made. In Chapter 5, Owner's Operating Expenses, we discussed an operating expense item, Repairs and Maintenance (a/k/a Reserves for Replacement or Replacement Reserve). This is a contingent fund of money set aside for emergency repairs. **If this money is not spent in a given year it needs to be added back to the income before calculating income taxes.**

The adjustment would appear as follows:

Net Operating Income

+ Reserves for Replacement

= Adjusted NOI

- Mortgage Interest

- Annual Depreciation

= Taxable Income

X Marginal Tax Rate

= Income Tax

Once the income tax has been calculated the After Tax Cash Flow may be determined.

Note: other deductions may further reduce the Taxable Income and the property may be eligible for certain Tax Credits. Always check with an accountant or tax advisor.

The complete financial analysis is reflected by this chart:

Potential Rental Income

Plus Additional Income from Tenants

Less Vacancy and Credit Losses

Equals Effective Rental Income (sub-total)

Plus Other Building Income

Equals Gross Operating Income

Less Owners Operating Expenses

Equals Net Operating Income (NOI)

Less Annual Debt Service (when financed)

Equals Cash Flow Before Taxes (CFBT)

Less Income Tax

Equals Cash Flow After Taxes (CFAT)

Let's look at an example which will tie together many of the concepts previously discussed. We will use the Office Building Case Study from Chapters 5 and 6.

Potential Rental Income	$125,000
Plus Additional Income from Tenants	5,000
Less Vacancy and Credit Losses	- 6,500
Equals Effective Rental Income (sub-total)	123,500
Plus Other Building Income	6,000
Equals Gross Operating Income	129,500
Less Owners Operating Expenses	47,475
Equals Net Operating Income (NOI)	$ 82,025

In Chapter 6 we determined the value of this building to be $1,093,667. Let us consider purchasing the building today for $1,000,000; financing the property with a down payment of 30% ($300,000) and terms being a $700,000 loan, 7% interest, 20 year term.

The Annual Debt Service would be $65,125. The first year's amortization would show of that, $16,653 was paid on the principal of the loan and $48,472 was paid on the mortgage interest.

Before proceeding further, let us also make sure the loan would meet today's underwriting standards for a Debt Service Ratio is 1.25 or higher.

$$\frac{NOI}{ADS} = DSR \qquad \frac{\$82,025}{\$65,125} = 1.26$$

Continuing:

Net Operating Income (NOI)	$82,025
Less Annual Debt Service (when financed)	-65,125
Equals Cash Flow Before Taxes (CFBT)	$16,900

Next the Income Tax must be calculated:

To do so the depreciation must be determined. Land does not depreciate. We will assume a land value of 20% of the price for this example.

$1,000,000 less 20% land value $200,000, building value is $800,000.

This is an Office Building, the depreciation schedule is 39 years, and therefore the depreciation deduction is $20,513 ($800,000 ÷ 39 years).

Reminder, in calculating the Income Tax, if "Reserves for Replacement" was taken as a building expense and in fact those moneys were not spent that year the money must be added back in before the tax is calculated.

The Income Tax is calculated using the following sequence:
(For this example we will assume the taxpayer is in the 24% tax bracket.)

Net Operating Income	$82,025
+ Reserves for Replacement	6,475
= Adjusted NOI	88,500
- Mortgage Interest	- 48,472
- Annual Depreciation	-20,513
= Taxable Income	19,515
X Marginal Tax Rate	24%
= Income Tax	$4,684

We may now conclude our analysis:

Net Operating Income (NOI)	$82,025
Less Annual Debt Service (when financed)	-65,125
Equals Cash Flow Before Taxes (CFBT)	16,900
Less Income Tax	- 4,684
Equals Cash Flow After Taxes (CFAT)	$12,216

This is a complete analysis of the properties cash flows, demonstrating current NOI, typical financing and underwriting, and showing the impact of depreciation in determining the real return on this investment (after the income taxes have been paid).

The CFAT is also measured as the **Return on Equity**. Investors will compare various opportunities based upon the first years Return on Equity. In this case:

$$\frac{\text{Cash Flow After Taxes}}{\text{Initial Investment}} = \text{Return on Equity}$$

$$\frac{\$12,216}{\$300,000} = .041 \quad (4\%)$$

They may also project forward their Return on Equity based upon appreciation assumptions. Assuming as time goes on, the building will appreciate in value, and the mortgage principal is paid down their equity will increase.

In comparison, if this property were purchased for all cash, no debt service, no mortgage interest deduction:

Net Operating Income	$82,025
+ Reserves for Replacement	6,475
= Adjusted NOI	88,500
- Annual Depreciation	-20,513
= Taxable Income	67,987
X Marginal Tax Rate	24%
= Income Tax	$16,397

Net Operating Income (NOI)	$82,025
Cash Flow Before Taxes (CFBT) is the NOI	82,025
Less Income Tax	-16,397
Equals Cash Flow After Taxes (CFAT)	$65,628

$$\frac{\text{Cash Flow After Taxes}}{\text{Purchase Price}} = \text{Return on Investment}$$

$$\frac{\$65,628}{\$1,000,000} = 6.60\%$$

Investments show different returns base upon several factors, the tax bracket of the owner, and when financed the amount of debt and the terms of the loan.

In the above comparison the owner may have $1,000,000 to invest, they may buy one building with it or create several down payments to invest in multiple building by leveraging their money. In which case, we would need to examine the cumulative return on all those investments to have a fare comparison. Individual investors may thoroughly examine "the numbers" right down to their After Tax Cash Flow and percentage of Return on Investment based on their specific tax bracket.

All income tax matters should be reviewed by an accountant or tax advisor.

Part 6

Being a Landlord

Chapter 15: Introduction to Leases

Your goal in being a landlord is to keep you building totally occupied to maximize your cash flow. How much money an owner can make on an investment property is largely influenced by their contracts with their tenants, known as **Leases**.

When space becomes vacant you want to fill it as soon as possible. You may want to advertise the availabilities or hire a Commercial Real Estate Broker to do the marketing, screening of potential tenants, and initial negotiations for you. Generally, a Letter of Intent (LOI) will serve as an offer to lease your space, including many details. Once all the details are agreed then a formal Lease will be drafted, generally by your attorney.

In preparing to lease your property you need to determine what your position will be on various issues, all of this list and more will be discussed in detail in this and the other chapters in this section.

What is your position?

Acceptable uses (per zoning code, your desired uses, any other tenant restrictions)?

Building access hours open?

Tenant Improvements? Would you allow? Would you pay for?

Type of lease, Gross, Net, NNN, Percentage, other?

Term of the lease (length)? Option to renew (extend)? Option to expand?

If Office, measurement of space, Net Usable, Rentable, Loss Factor?

Base rent? Additional rent? Utilities? CAM Charges?

Taxes, who pays, how calculated?

Escalations (rent increases)?

Amount of Security Deposit?

Are you offering concessions or abatements of rent?

Insurance requirements?

Who is responsible for repairs and maintenance?

Purchase Option?

Are you requiring Personal Guarantees?

Is Signage Available?

Parking, assigned spaces, additional charges?

Sub-lease or Assignment clauses?

Green lease clauses?

Is your building ADA Compliant?

What Security features does your building have, cameras, guards?

Leases

A lease is a binding contract and it is strongly recommended that an attorney be employed to draft or review leases.

"Standard" leases can be purchased at stationary or office supply stores or a "Standard" lease may have been created for a large building owner twenty years ago and is still being used today. A "standard" lease is considered to be slanted heavily in favor of the landlord. In reality there should be no standard lease, as each transaction, each negotiation is different.

In some cases a standard lease form may be used; this may be referred to as the "boilerplate" agreement. However a second document may be added known as the "Rider". The rider changes, modifies or eliminates certain clauses or terms in the boilerplate document. Anything in the rider supersedes anything in the original lease.

Typical language that may begin a rider:

"Provisions of this rider are hereby incorporated into and made a part of the lease dated…between…If there are any conflicts between the provisions of the rider and the remainder of the lease, the provisions of the rider shall govern."

In an ideal situation a lease should be like a business partnership between the landlord and the tenant. It should be fair and reasonable to both parties.

A lease specifically indicates who is responsible for what and who pays for what. It is essential that the lease covers all possible issues and circumstances; that there are no "grey" areas that could cause future disputes and litigation.

It is strongly recommended that leases be drafted and reviewed by attorneys who specialize in commercial real estate.

Typical Types of Leases:

Gross Lease - The landlord collects rent from the tenants and from the money collected pays all the operating expenses of the building. In some cases, the landlord collects rent from the tenant and "passes through" to the tenant additional costs representative of certain of the buildings expenses. In this case we would refer to the lease as a **Modified Gross Lease,** for example, the cost of power or utilities. The rent may be quoted as $30 PSF base rent plus $2.50 PSF for the cost of utilities.

Triple Net (NNN) Lease – The name of this type of lease is very deceptive; it implies three things. It is in fact the other extreme to the gross lease, in the Triple Net Lease the tenant pays rent to the landlord <u>and the tenant also pays all (or their proportionate share) of the building operating costs.</u>

The Triple Net Lease is sometimes written with a structural exclusion. A leaking roof repair may be the responsibility of the tenant, but if the entire roof needs replacement that would be the landlord's expense.

Net Lease – This type of lease is considered to fall between the gross and triple net leases in that the Net Lease means the landlord will pay some of the building operating expenses and the tenant will pay some of the operating costs. The lease will clearly define who is responsible for what and who will pay for what.

It is important, as we assign responsibility for payment of operating expenses, that this be fair and accountable. A landlord may pass through to a tenant their proportionate share of the electric or fuel costs; the tenant should have the right to review the actual

bills for accuracy. The tenant pays additional rent of $2.50 per square foot for utilities; the lease should allow the tenant to review the basis of this cost and also allow the landlord to periodically adjust the cost based upon the actual expenses.

A **Flat Lease** means that the amount of rent will not increase during the term of the lease. As one might expect this would usually apply to a relatively short term lease. This is also known as a **month-to-month lease.** (Even if the term of a lease is short a written document detailing all the terms is appropriate). This type of lease may occur when someone is moving and their new space is not ready, necessitating a short term lease elsewhere; or for seasonal businesses.

A **Step-Up or Graduated Lease** establishes a base rent, but reduces the initial rent due for a period of time. For example the stores rent will be $2,000 per month, but to help the tenant get started (or build up a client base) the landlord aggress to $1,000 per month for the first three month, $1,500 per month for the next three months and then in the seventh month of the lease the full rent commences. Often child care facilities are new construction and they can not get their state license until the building is completed and a Certificate of Occupancy is obtained. Consequently they can not register any children until licensed. This type of lease gives them time to complete their enrollment, and develop their regular cash flow before the full rent is due.

Ground or Land Leases - As it sounds the tenant is renting the land and the tenant is responsible to make any desired improvements (like constructing a building) at their own expense. Since the tenant is doing the improvement they want a long lease to get the benefits of their construction and amortize their cost. Hence land leases today are generally written for a 49 year term (in the past many were written for a 99 year term). These types of leases are generally "triple net" whereby the tenant pays all the expenses, real estate taxes, insurance, etc. The rent is increased, but usually in five year increments.

Build-to-Suit - In this case there is generally a developer who finds a property (vacant or with a building on it that may be demolished) they think would be good for a national company. They approach the national company with a proposal that they will construct a building per their plans and specifications on the site. In exchange they expect a long term lease to be signed (20 years or more). The rent and escalations are negotiated and the lease is signed. The developer **builds-to-suit** the building and the tenant moves in. Then the developer sells the entire project to an investor and looks to do the same type of project again for someone else.

Turnkey Lease - This is very similar to the build-to-suit, but goes a step further. Tenants who seek these leases want the developer to do everything in terms of finishing the space. This could include painting, wallpapering, building fixtures, providing furnishings so that on the date of occupancy the tenant could literally turn the key in the door and go to work. Obviously this extra work is going to cost more and the rent will be higher.

Sale-Leaseback A successful business owner may need cash for expansion, another facility or other investment. They own the building their business operates out of generally without debt. To raise capital they sell their building to an investor becoming the tenant. The deal may be something like this: If you buy my building for $1,000,000; I will become the tenant and offer you an 8% return on your investment and a long term lease (i.e. 20 years). This would be a Triple Net lease with a base rent of $80,000 a year. The seller gets their capital and the investor gets a stable tenant with a good return on their investment. This is quite popular in the industrial manufacturing sector.

Percentage Leases apply only to retail businesses. In this case part of the rent paid to the landlord is a percentage of the sales of the retailer. The percentage may apply to all sales from day one of the lease or more commonly a "breakeven" point is established.

Retailers often look at their business year, anticipating all the expenses for the year and consequently consider the year starting off without profit. However a point in time is reached where the store starts to make a profit for the year. Given this concept, in a Percentage Lease a breakeven or threshold dollar amount is determined and the percentage is negotiated. After sales reach the breakeven point the tenant pays as additional rent the agreed percentage of all sales thereafter.

When creating a breakeven point a formula is used:

Key Formula:

$$\frac{\textbf{Annual Rent}}{\textbf{Percentage of Sales}} = \textbf{"Breakeven Point"}$$

The "Breakeven Point" is a dollar amount of sales, after which the tenant must remit the percentage of sales to the landlord as additional rent.

For Example:

A tenant's base rent is $5,000 per month or $60,000 a year. The tenant also agrees to a Percentage Lease and to pay 5% of their sales after reaching a Breakeven Point.

$$\frac{\$60,000}{5\%} = \$1,200,000$$

Once the store sales reach $1,200,000 the tenant will pay 5% of all future sales to the landlord in addition to the monthly base rent of $5,000.

Sublease This begins as a clause in the original lease that would allow the tenant to rent out part or all of their space. The clause would require the landlords consent and approval. When this is done a second lease is constructed between the Tenant, now referred to as the Master Tenant and the Sub-Tenant. There is no direct contractual relationship between the Sub-Tenant and the Landlord. The Sub-Tenant pays their rent to the Master Tenant who in turn pays the Landlord. The original Tenant is liable under the lease for all rent due.

Sandwich Leasehold – This is a funny term that refers to a Sublease. The idea being that the tenant is "sandwiched" between the landlord and sub-tenant.

The "Green" Lease – For a period of time, leases just added "green clauses" on a best efforts basis. Landlord and Tenant agree to recycle, agree to shut off lights; to make an effort to conserve energy and help the environment. Now there are actual "green leases", with specific clauses covering many aspects of the lease.

For example, this is the typical Sublease and Assignment Clause, "Tenant shall not sublease all or any part of the Leased Premises, or assign this Lease in whole or in part without Landlord's consent, such consent not to be unreasonably withheld or delayed."

The Sublease and Assignment Clause in a Green Lease, "The landlord may insist that its consent to a proposed assignment or sublease can reasonably be denied in the event the proposed assignee or subtenant will or could cause part or all of the building not to conform in accordance with green aspects of the lease, including the third-party certification system."

The basic concept in the Green Lease is to mandate the Landlord and Tenant to work together to maintain and improve the energy efficiencies in the building and if a "rating" was earned to continue it.

Chapter 16: Measuring Space

How much space does the tenant get to use or occupy, and is it always the same amount of space that they have to pay for? No.

We measure space in square footage. Then the rent is calculated either on an annual or a monthly basis depending on your market. I am in the Northeast and generally the rental cost is quoted as the annual cost per square foot; in other parts of the country it is quoted as the monthly cost per foot.

Space is measured differently in various types of buildings. In some smaller building owners simply measure the inside dimensions and that is what the tenant is billed for.

Office buildings, however, are often large with multiple tenants. Landlords desire to be paid for "every square inch" of their building. In these properties tenants get to exclusively occupy and use a certain amount of space but they also share "common areas" with all the other tenants in the building. So a tenant ends up occupying **Net or Usable Square Footage** but paying for this space plus their proportionate share of the common area, known as the **Rentable or Gross or Billable Square Footage.** Different terms are used in different areas and by various landlords.

Important Concept:

Tenants often have to pay for more space than they occupy.

How is space measured? The general authority on space measurement is **BOMA,** the **Building Owners and Managers Association**. Generally, a building is looked at in three ways. Certain parts of the building are considered "structural" and would be included in the base rental charge. For example: Thickness of exterior walls, exterior balconies, mechanical penthouse, upper stories of atriums, and major vertical penetrations (staircases, elevator shafts).

The tenant occupied unit square footage is measured from the inside of the walls within the unit and includes all usable space and storage areas. If there are demising walls, internal walls dividing the space, like a private office, that space is included. Tenants must absorb HVAC convectors, columns and interior building projections in their measurements.

The **common areas** of a building may consist of lobbies and atriums (at floor level), public corridors (and include the thickness of the corridor walls), public restrooms, janitor, electric and phone closets, mechanical rooms, and loading docks. Such measurements will include the "common areas" on all floors.

When a building is constructed an architect or engineer will measure all the space in the building and determine the overall amount of usable square footage and the amount of common area square footage. The percentage difference between the Usable and Rentable space is known as the **Loss Factor or Core Factor.** For Example: a building is 100,000 SF in total space, 15,000 SF of that space is common area. The Loss or Core factor would be 15%.

Landlords are entitled to get paid for all the space in their buildings including the "common areas". There are different methods used to do this calculation, the most common ways are the **Add-On Factor** and the **Loss or Core Factor** method.

The **Add-On Factor** is generally found in use in areas where there is high vacancy and low absorption rates, where it take a long time to fill vacant space. It is best illustrated by example. A tenant can use and occupy 10,000 SF in a building. The landlord uses an Add-On factor of 15% representing the common area of the building. How much space is the tenant billed for?

To calculate; we consider the usable square footage occupied by the tenant to be 100% of their space and add to that 15%. The percentages are converted to decimals and multiplied by the usable amount of space.

100% + 15% = 115% or 1.15

10,000 SF X 1.15 = 11,500 SF

The tenant must pay for 11,500 SF of space.

Another method of measurement is the **Loss Factor or Core Factor** method of calculating **Rentable Square Footage a/k/a Gross Square Footage or Billable Square Footage.** This system of calculation is found in use in areas of generally low vacancy and relatively high absorption rates, where space rents relatively quickly. In this method the landlord advises the Net or Usable Square Footage and the Loss or Core Factor percentage. The Rentable Square Footage is then calculated according to this formula:

Key Formula:

$$\frac{\text{Net Square Footage}}{1 - \text{Loss Factor Percentage}} = \text{Rentable Square Footage}$$

To determine the denominator for this equation we subtract from the whole number 1 (one), the loss factor percentage as a decimal, this gives us the inverse of the loss factor.

For example: The landlord advises the usable square footage is 1,000 SF and the building has a 20% Loss Factor.

Step 1: Calculate the inverse of the loss factor (denominator for the equation)

20% = .20

1 - .20 = .8

Step 2: Calculate the Rentable Square Footage using the formula

$$\frac{1,000 \text{ Net SF}}{.8} = 1,250 \text{ Rentable SF}$$

Note, in contrast if the Add-On Formula were used for this calculation the result would be 1,200 SF

100% + 20% = 120% or 1.20

1,000 SF X 1.20 = 1,200 SF

The result of using the Loss Factor or Core Factor method is more space is allocated to the tenant; consequently more money to the landlord.

Retail Properties

Measuring space in retail properties, where there is only one tenant, is done from the exterior of the building, including the thickness of the exterior walls.

When measuring a store in a "strip centers", the structure is considered. Strip centers are usually constructed as a large rectangular building divided into six or ten or more stores. In this case the landlord also wants to be paid for every square inch of space.

When measuring these stores, as to how much space the tenant must pay for, the exterior walls and the proportionate share of walls dividing the stores are included. The tenant will pay for the space they occupy measured from the outside of the exterior walls plus half the thickness of the walls that divide them from the adjacent stores.

There can be exceptions, measuring space in retail properties may also be done including a loss factor or add-on factor if we have enclosed shopping centers or malls with common areas. Generally, small "Main Street" stores are measured using the inside dimensions only.

Industrial Properties

Many industrial properties have only one tenant and they pay rent based on the entire square footage of the building, measured from the exterior of the walls. When there are multiple tenants measuring is done the same as retail. The tenant will pay for the space they occupy measured from the exterior walls plus half the thickness of any walls that divide them from the adjacent units.

Chapter 17: Lease Clauses

A lease gives the right of possession to a tenant in the owners building for a period of time. A good lease needs to address every possible situation that may arise while the tenant is in the building, so it is clearly understood what the tenant may or may not do, who is responsible for what and who pays for what. We will look at some common clauses and things to consider, **but to protect yourself seek legal advice before entering into any contract (lease) whether you are a landlord or a tenant.** Following are some typical lease clauses; others may be required based on circumstances. Not all clauses are necessary for every situation.

Use Clause

What is a permitted use of the space? There may be some local zoning regulations that dictate what a building can or cannot be used for. Check with the local building department first.

In the lease a definition of the permitted use is important. Generally owners want this to be as restrictive as possible, but tenants want the definition as broad as possible.

Example: A tenant wants to open a Shoe Store in a 10 store shopping center. From the tenant point of view they intend to sell shoes and related articles; sox, hosiery and perhaps handbags. The more related articles the better chance they have of being successful. But the landlord considers what if another store becomes vacant. If this store is restricted to only shoe sales, then I could rent the other store to a firm that just sells hosiery or handbags.

Consider a tenant, restricted to just selling shoes, who needs to expand to a larger location before their lease expires. Their lease may permit them to sub-lease (defined later in this chapter) their space but they could only sub-lease the space to their competition, another shoe store.

Under the best of circumstances this tenant's use would be defined as "sale of shoes or any other legally permitted products". This would allow them to sell related items in their store and in the event they had to sub-lease they could do so to a different business.

Use Restrictions

Landlords sometimes allow use restrictions to be in leases. In a small strip center a lease is entered into with a tenant for a Pizza Parlor. The lease specifies that no other store in the strip may be another Pizza Parlor.

In larger centers there may be an "Anchor" tenant, typically a supermarket or a department store. In the case of a supermarket there could be a restriction that none of the smaller stores may be a bakery or butcher shop as those goods are sold in the supermarket.

When does the lease start?

Leases may have three or more different "trigger dates". The day the lease is signed is known as the lease **Commencement Date**. There will also be an **Occupancy Date** when the tenant will take possession of the space. This will depend upon several things, is the space currently vacant and does any work need to be done prior to occupancy. The third date is the **Rent Commencement Date,** at what point does the tenant start paying rent? A **Rent Concession** or an **Abatement Period** is a period of free rent, which may have been negotiated.

Another consideration, what if the space is currently occupied by another tenant who cannot move out on time? If construction is required before occupancy, what if the space is not available on time? This can be a major problem. The new tenant may have additional moving expenses or may have to move into temporary quarters and effectively have to move twice.

The lease may need a contingency clause to address this, i.e. the rent commencement date shall be abated (delayed) until actual occupancy. But, tenants may also want the additional costs or moving expenses paid by the landlord in the event of delay. To offset some of the possible costs most leases have a **Holdover Clause** which states in the event the tenant does not move out, on time, at the expiration of the lease, the monthly rent is doubled or tripled for any time they remain in the space.

Defining the Rent

The lease must clearly indicate the amount space the tenant must pay for (prior chapter) the **Rentable Square Footage or Gross or Billable Square Footage**. Based upon this calculation the exact amount of rent due each month and each year for the full term of the lease must be stated. Rent increase or escalations for subsequent years are included in this calculation. The amount of rent so stated is known as the **Base Rent**. There may be **Additional Rent** also charged to the tenant in the form of "pass thru's".

Rent Escalations

The concept of escalating or increasing the rent is based upon keeping up with inflation or changes in market conditions (values) resulting from supply and demand. Therefore the geographic location of the property and the economics of that area indicate what annual rent increases are appropriate. Also in a case where the landlord is paying all or many of the operating costs of the buildings this increase is used to offset the anticipated increase in those expenses. **It is generally not a profit center for the landlord.**

The lease will define any increases in the rent during the term of the lease. If the increase is a specific percentage the percentage of increase will be stated and typically a chart will show the exact amount of rent due each year and each month of the lease term.

For example a five-year lease with 4% annual rent escalations:

Base Rent

January 1 – December 31, Year1	$24,000.00 Year	$2,000.00 Month
January 1 – December 31, Year 2	$24,960.00 Year	$2,080.00 Month
January 1 – December 31, Year 3	$25,958.40 Year	$2,163.20 Month
January 1 – December 31, Year 4	$26,996.74 Year	$2,249.73 Month
January 1 - December 31, Year 5	$28,076.61 Year	$2,339.72 Month

Increases do not have to be annual. In longer leases the increase may be every four or five years (usually a higher percentage).

The lease needs to be as specific as possible so there are no misunderstandings as to rental obligations.

Cost of Living Increases– Consumers Price Indexes

Another method if increasing rent is based upon **"cost of living" increases**. For example if the cost of living increases in an area by 3%, this would be the increase imposed upon the tenants.

Using this method requires further definition. Which cost of living index will be used? There are many different statistical reports produced reflecting changes in the cost of living. Some are based upon figures for the entire United States, some regional North East, South West, and some for major metropolitan areas New York, Chicago or San Francisco. A common report used is the **Consumers Price Index (CPI)** issued by the U.S. Department of Labor, Bureau of Labor Statistics (www.bls.gov). Even using the CPI requires further definition of which CPI index. Common choices include the CPI All Urban Consumers or the CPI Urban Wage Earners & Clerical Workers. Using this method of increasing rent also requires a time definition as these reports are produced monthly. "The latest monthly increase on the anniversary date of the lease…" "The increase will be based on the average CPI (name of report) increase for the prior calendar year."

Using any cost of living index is a gamble for both the landlord and tenant. Educated guesses of future increases can be made but the economy could change. It is not uncommon when a cost of living increase is used for the tenant to request a CAP, a maximum percentage increase that may be applied. The rent shall increase based upon the CPI, not to exceed an increase of 4.5% per year.

Pass Thru Clauses

Reference has been made to passing through (thru) various expenses to the tenant. Care needs to be taken in defining within the lease how and when this is to be done.

For example there is one source of power to a building and ten tenants. Does each tenant pay $1/10^{th}$ of the monthly electric bill? If they each occupy equal space in the building, that may be feasible. However, if different size units were rented breaking down the expense proportionately would seem appropriate. Then, in the lease, the percentage of the building being occupied by that tenant needs to be defined. "Tenant A

154

is responsible to pay 12% of all electric charges to the building, to be billed on a monthly basis."

Another method of billing is to take the annual (historical) cost of an expense and divide the expense by the overall square footage of the building determining a cost per square foot. For example, the rent is $25.00 PSF plus $2.25 PSF for utilities. Each tenant is billed according to the space they rent. With this method the lease must define how this fee is initially determined and make provision for periodic revision and adjustment if the expense increases or decreases. This is especially important when Utility, Electric, or CAM Charges (Common Area Maintenance) are passed through to a tenant. Each charge included in this category must also be defined. "CAM charges will be reviewed and reassessed on a quarterly basis."

Pass thru's may also apply to unexpected increases in a certain expense. The lease would establish a CAP or threshold for that expense and the tenant would pay their proportionate share of the expense when the cost exceeds the CAP. For example, the landlord agrees to provide heat to the tenants. The building is heated with fuel oil. But if the cost of the oil exceeds $2.50 per gallon, the tenants must pay their share of the increased cost.

Real Estate Tax Pass Thru

The buildings Real Estate Taxes may be paid by the Landlord, or proportionately paid by the Tenant. I.e. The tenant occupies 12 % of the building; they pay 12% of the real estate taxes. The tenant's contribution to the tax bill is due and payable upon receipt of the annual or semi-annual tax bill. Clarification as to how and when this is to be paid must also be defined in the lease.

Tax Escalation Clause a/k/a Tax Stop Clause is an alternative way taxes are handled in many office buildings (but, could be applied to any type of building). The Landlord agrees to pay the real estate taxes based upon the present taxes on the day the lease is signed. If the taxes go up after that date the tenant is responsible to pay their proportionate share of the increase.

Options

Some leases give the tenant an option to extend (or renew) their lease, at predetermined rates. If this is so, the exact dollars are entered into the lease. The lease should include a chart showing the rent due per year and month for the entire term..

For example:

The lease is a **five-year term with a five-year option** (to renew or extend the lease). Increases will be 3% per year during the **base term** (first five-year primary term) and if the option is exercised the rent will increase by 4% with 4% annual increases thereafter.

Base Term (3% annual increases)

January 1 – December 31, Year1	$24,000.00 Year	$2,000.00 Month
January 1 – December 31, Year 2	$24,720.00 Year	$2,060.00 Month
January 1 – December 31, Year 3	$25,461.60 Year	$2,121.80 Month
January 1 – December 31, Year 4	$26,225.45 Year	$2,185.45 Month
January 1 - December 31, Year 5	$27,012.21 Year	$2,251.02 Month

Option Period (4% annual increases)

January 1 – December 31, Year 6	$28,092.70 Year	$2,341.06 Month
January 1 – December 31, Year 7	$29,216.41 Year	$2,434.70 Month
January 1 – December 31, Year 8	$30,385.06 Year	$2,532.09 Month
January 1 – December 31, Year 9	$31,600.47 Year	$2,633.37 Month
January 1 - December 31, Year 10	$32,864.49 Year	$2,738.71 Month

In some cases an Extension Option is granted but the rent for the option period is not negotiated at the time the lease is signed. Sometimes an amount of money to **exercise the option** is required. For example, "In order to exercise the option to continue the lease for an additional five years there will be a fee of $10,000."

As the Landlord you are under no obligation to give a tenant an option to renew or extend the lease, this is negotiable. However in granting the option or options (you may have a five year lease with four five year options to renew), this often assists in tenant retention. On the down side what if market conditions change dramatically and five years later rent are much higher than what was agreed to in the option period.

Landlords Note

Options give the tenant a choice to stay for the extension period or to leave when the initial lease term is over. Landlords are bound by all the options if the tenant chooses to exercise then. You are stuck with the tenant even if you do not like them or even if you could rent the space for more money at that time.

The lease needs to be as specific as possible so there are no misunderstandings as to rental obligations.

Any terms may be negotiated. The escalation rate may be the same, or change for the option period. Leases with cost of living escalations usually continue on that basis in the option periods, (with the rent being unknown no future rent due charts appear in these leases).

A **Flat Lease** may have no annual increases. But may have an increase for an option period; i.e. the lease is for two years with a two year option; the rent for the base term will be $50,000 per year; if the option is exercised the rent will increase 5% for the next two years.

Option to Buy

Some leases will afford the tenant an option to buy the building. If a specific time period (relatively short, i.e. within two years) is given to do so, the price to buy will usually be stated in the lease.

Dual Appraisal Method

In long leases an option to buy may be offered. But this may be exercised many years in the future and what the fair market value of the building will be at that time is unknown. To determine market value at a future time the Dual Appraisal Method is used. The landlord and the tenant each obtain an appraisal of property value. The lease may even require a Commercial Appraiser be used, sometimes requiring someone with the MAI (Member Appraisal Institute) Designation. The appraisals should both be "close in value" and this is used as the basis to set price. Often the lease language contains a procedure for a third appraisal or a method to settle the value if in dispute.

Right of First Refusal (ROFR)

Some tenants will request a Right of First Refusal. If during the term of the lease the owner decides to sell the property they would have an opportunity to purchase it. This gives the tenant this right, but also is a method to establish the price. The way it works is the property is placed on the market for sale, a purchase offer is made by a third party (presumably at fair market value). The tenant with the ROFR must match the purchase offer exactly (dollars and terms) then they may buy the building.

First Opportunity Clause

A tenant may feel in the future they will need to lease additional space in your building. They may request, when new space becomes available in the building, to be given the first opportunity to lease that additional space. The cost for that additional space may also be included in this clause. Typically that the rent be the same as the tenant is paying at that time or state the rent will be Fair Market Value. This is done to protect the tenant from having the landlord inflate the rental value at that time.

Building Insurance

Certain events may be protected as result of perils covered under an insurance policy. **Understanding insurance coverage is important for a landlord.** Typically a landlord carries a "fire" insurance policy (that covers other disasters as well) on the building that would pay to replace or repair the building in such a catastrophe. The lease usually holds harmless the landlord for any of the tenants "possessions", making it the tenants responsibility to carry their own insurance to protect their property and business interruption in the event of fire or other event.

Besides reconstructing the building in the event of fire or another major disaster, the owner needs a form of business interruption insurance. Such catastrophes may permit tenants to suspend rent payment or even terminate their leases, yet the mortgage payment on the building may continue to be due. Insurance policies are needed that will replace lost cash flow in such circumstances.

Investment Tip: Be sure to have a Structural Engineer examine any building you are considering purchasing.

Protecting Yourself

Liability issues come with owning a building, especially if you have tenants in the building. Accidents do occur which sometimes develop into lawsuits. Even if an incident occurred in a tenant space, the building owner could also get sued.

Important Concept:

Speak with an attorney to determine the best form of ownership for you. It may be prudent to have the building owned by a Corporation, LLC (Limited Liability Corporation) or another type of entity.

Liability Insurance

The owner of a property may carry his or her own liability insurance. As a practical application of insurance there are comprehensive policies that provide a building owner with a combination of fire, other perils, business interruption and liability protections.

In addition to their own coverage the owner may have a lease clause that requiring the tenant to carry insurance with the amounts of coverage for property damage and liability stated. Further, as an added protection to the landlord, a tenant insurance policy should call for the building owner to be added as **"an additional named insured"**. This term means that any notifications from the insurance company to the tenant (policy holder) must be copied to the landlord, i.e. any premium past due notice, lapse or termination of coverage. The insurance clauses usually also require that a copy of the insurance policy or a **"Certificate of Insurance"** be given to the Landlord.

Important Concept:

Insurance can be a major expense to a landlord. While considering the purchase of an investment building get several quotes of building insurance.

Tenant Improvements (TI)

A major area of negotiations is construction or improvements within the space the tenant will occupy. There are two issues will the landlord allow proposed changes to the building or unit and who will pay the costs of the construction?

When a tenant considers leasing space in a building usually a **Letter of Intent (LOI)** is submitted to the landlord. This is a proposal to lease the space and defines the terms the tenant desires or that have been agreed upon. If there is a request for construction a detailed sketch or drawing is attached. This is referred to as a request for **Tenant Improvements, TI, a "build out" or "work letter".** It could be relatively simple, landlord to provide two 10' x 10' private offices within the unit, or much more complicated. The landlord will determine if they will allow such changes, and if so the cost of the improvements. Then negotiations begin on who will pay for the work.

Sometimes a landlord recognizes that the space offered will require work and offers a **Tenant Improvement Allowance,** indicating they will pay for the tenant cost of construction up to a dollar limit, i.e. $4,000. This could also be stated as a Tenant Improvement Allowance of $4.00 PSF.

Restoration Fund

Another issue that may arise is the requested work would not be suitable for future tenants. Consider a telemarketing operation. The tenant wants to have 50 small cubicles constructed in the unit and even offers to pay for the construction themselves. This may suit this tenants needs but the landlord realizes that most businesses would not be able to use the space this way. When this tenants lease is over it will be necessary to remove this structure to make the space attractive to a new tenant.

The landlord may agree to this construction provided that the tenant, at their own expense, removes the structures and return the space to the condition that it was in

161

prior to the construction. Language to this effect would be contained in the lease agreement. Beyond this however, the landlord may seek further protection and require the establishment of a **"restoration fund"**. Money equal to the cost of returning the space to pre-lease condition that would be held by the landlord to use in the event of a default by the tenant.

Repair and Maintenance

The lease will define the responsibilities of the landlord and tenant to maintain the quality of the building and its mechanical systems. Also if something goes wrong in the building who is responsible for the repair. If the repair is the borne by the tenant and such repair is not made in a timely fashion, generally the lease will permit the landlord to make such necessary repair and charge the tenant the cost of such repairs. Leases usually contain another clause for the opposite situation whereby the landlord is responsible for a repair and if it is not made the tenant may make such repairs and deduct the cost from their rent.

Hours of Operation

Leases will define the hours the building is open.

In a retail situation we may have local regulations restricting hours. Stores are closed on Sundays or no 24 hour businesses are permitted. In the case of a shopping center it may be required that all stores be open 10:00 am to 9:00 pm Monday thru Saturday and open 10:00 am to 6:00 pm on Sundays.

In office situations, especially larger buildings, the building may be opened at 7:00 am and locked down at 7:00 pm, with limited access on weekends. Often if a tenant needs to work late occasionally, there could be a charge for the overtime use of services, as the landlord would then need to keep the light, heat, air, etc. operating.

Lease Details

A good lease will address all possible issues between the landlord and the tenant. In this section we are only highlighting some of the possible issues and clauses. All details must be discussed and resolved. Some items seem simple but have "hidden" costs.

Signs – Will the landlord give the tenant permission to have a sign on the building? This "yes or no" question needs further clarification. If yes, what size will be allowed? Are there any local laws to be considered? Subject to landlord approval of design? Who is going to pay for the actual sign to be created? Who is going to pay to have the sign installed on the building?

Parking – Are any assigned parking spaces being given to the tenant? Where in the parking lot are they located? If the tenant wants assigned parking spaces is there an additional charge?

The Bad Tenant

Selection of tenants is done with as much care and information as possible, but after a tenant is in the building things may occur that affect their business. One day they are gone! The lease has been broken and the space they occupied is a disaster. Two situations need to be addressed; the cash flow of the building needs to be restored, and legal issues from the tenant defaulting on the lease. A lease needs to address all these possibilities to protect the landlord.

The space needs to be leased to a new tenant. That means making repairs and fixing the space, with these costs now being borne by the landlord. Obtaining **Security Deposits** as part of the lease process can perhaps help offset some of the costs. There are two categories of loss to consider, the physical rehabbing of the space and the "down time" loss of rent until a new tenant is found and their lease commences. Typically security deposits are one, two or three months rent and this amount may not be sufficient to cover such losses. It may be difficult to request a large security deposit but **"risk"** (of default) must be considered when selecting tenants. A realistic approach to "what is my worst case scenario" may be prudent in determining security deposits. If the space goes vacant what would it cost to repaint, fix up etc. and how long would it take to get a new tenant paying rent? The amount of security deposit could also vary based upon the financials of the potential tenant. Are they a **"Credit Worthy"** or **"Credit Rated"** company – a regional or national firm or public company?

Be aware some States have specific regulations regarding the holding of security deposits. This may involve how and where the funds are held, the co-mingling of accounts and who gets the interest. **Be sure to check local laws regarding holding security deposits.**

National Franchises - Care needs to be taken when dealing with National Franchises. Often the franchisee signs the lease and may even establish a new company to do so. **Do not assume the parent company will be signing the lease.** It may be possible to have the parent company guarantee the lease by the franchisee, or not!

Legal Remedies for Default

Leases need to contain provisions to protect the landlord. "What if" the tenant does not pay the rent on time, stops paying rent or "disappears in the night". **Consult with an attorney** to have your lease address these and other legal situations. Include penalties for late rent payments, eviction procedures, bankruptcy by the tenant, how to collect rent due in the event of default.

Personal Guarantee

Today most landlords require personal guarantees plus a complete financial check on the business owner's assets to ensure the owner(s) has the finances to back up the guarantee. If the business fails the burden of paying the rent falls on the business owner(s) to personally pay the rent do they have the assets to do so? This can get very complicated if there is a Corporation involved, as all the corporate officers would need to provide personal guarantees.

Landlords

Require all potential tenants to submit three years financials for their business and three years of their personal tax returns with their Letters of Intent. Have your accountant review this data.

Sub-Leasing Clause

This clause allows the tenant to rent out part or all of their space. It require landlord consent and approval. Language in the lease generally states, "such approval can not be unreasonably withheld."

When this is done a second lease is constructed between the Tenant, now referred to as the Master Tenant and the Sub-Tenant. There is no direct contractual relationship between the Sub-Tenant and the Landlord. The Sub-Tenant pays their rent to the Master Tenant who in turn pays the Landlord. See the following relationship chart.

<u>**Primary Lease**</u>

Landlord

↕

Tenant

Direct relationship

<u>**Sub-Lease**</u>

Landlord

↕

(Master) Tenant

↕

Sub-Tenant

No direct relationship between the landlord and sub-tenant.

The original Tenant is liable under the lease for all rent due. If the amount of money collected from the sub-tenant is not sufficient to pay the obligation to the landlord, the original tenant must pay the difference.

But what if a profit can be made from the sub-tenancy? Often the lease will indicate that if a profit is made the profit goes to the landlord or is split between the landlord and the original tenant.

Sub-leasing space in a down market can be a real challenge. A 10 year lease was signed three years ago with current annual rent at $70,000. Presently rents are down 20%, competitive space today is being rented for $56,000 a year. The tenant may be able to find a sub-tenant but may have to subsidize the rent by $14,000 a year to meet their leasehold obligation.

Lease Buy Out

The tenant no longer wants the space, so what is the possibility of buying out of the lease obligation? Just to keep it simple, with no escalations, the overall obligation to the

landlord for the next seven years is $490,000 (7years X $70,000 annual rent). In many cases such buy-out's are discounted considering the present value of money. In this case if a discount rate of 8% were applied the present value of the obligation would be reduced to $364,445. Several major questions, can the tenant afford to do this? Perhaps for major corporations, but I don't see our Main Street tenants being able to do so. Why should the landlord discount the obligation? Granted it is a lot of money and most likely the landlord can rent the space in a reasonable period of time.

The real question is how is the market today; will the landlord be able to rent the space for the same rent, more rent or lower rent? When the market is good the Lease Buy Out gives the landlord more than sufficient money to lease the space without cash flow interruption.

The dilemma is when we are in a declining market and the new rent would be less rent than the current tenant is paying. Should the landlord make the tenant fulfill their obligation by sub-leasing and having to subsidize the rent? (Can the tenant even afford that?) But what if the landlord does not work out a release with the tenant and the tenant goes bankrupt? This creates serious considerations all around.

Other Clauses to Release a Tenant from a Lease

Different owners refer to clauses that release tenants with various terminologies. What one clause means to one owner or attorney may mean something different to another. Be sure to clarify in detail when someone speaks of any of the following.

"Bail Out Clause" – This is often requested by National Retailers; if they open in a new location they hope their store will do very well and if so they would want to remain at that location for a long time. But if their market research in selecting that location were wrong and the store was not doing well they would want to terminate the lease.

They may request a lease with a five year term and four five year options, allowing them to stay there for twenty-five years if the store continues to perform well. But they may also request a **Bail Out Clause** after three years, to protect them if the store fails. Why would a landlord even consider doing this? Obviously, to hopefully have a National Tenant for a long time. But as to the Bail Out, they would require a significant penalty if it were exercised, typically one years' rent. This would give them sufficient time to replace the tenant without any interruption to their cash flow.

"Good Guy Clause" – This clause may take several forms. A landlord may simply agree to release a tenant if requested. The clause states: that in the event that the tenant has to break the lease, the tenant will notify the landlord, pay their rent up until the date they vacate the space, vacate the space and return the keys.

Sometimes the landlord agrees to do so but imposes a financial penalty for doing so.

In another form of Good Guy Clause the landlord may agree to release a tenant if the tenant can find a replacement tenant willing to pay equal or greater rent than they are paying. The landlord will need to approve this new tenant, their concern being that the new tenants financial strength or "credit worthiness" is equal to or greater than the current tenant. This puts the burden on the current tenant to find a replacement. If a Real Estate Broker is engaged to help find a new tenant the commission expense will be on the tenant.

Assignment

A lease may allow the tenant to assign the lease to another party, subject to landlord approval. Here the Assignee takes over the lease and has a direct relationship with the landlord. They must abide by all the terms and conditions of the lease. However the original tenant continues to have a liability for the leasehold obligation. If the assignee does not pay the rent or in any other way breaches the lease the original tenant is responsible.

Assignments of leases often result from the sale of a tenants business and consequent desire by the tenant to be completely removed from the lease responsibilities. The tenant who is assigning a lease generally desires to be released from any further liability. So often accompanying the assignment clause will be a **Release of Liability** clause. This requires the original tenant to pay a substantial penalty (perhaps six months' rent or more) to be released from the lease.

Non-Disturbance Clause

When a building is sold, the buyer must abide by all leases that are currently in effect for the remaining term of those lease and any option periods. However, if a building is **foreclosed** on by a bank or other financial institution, the foreclosing entity may terminate any or all of the leases.

Tenants, especially large or National tenants and those who may have spent considerable money on improvements will want to remain in the building and not have their leases terminated. They will request the lease have a **Non-Disturbance Clause**. This states that in the event of foreclosure, providing the tenant is not in default of their rent payments, the foreclosing entity may not terminate their lease. This needs to be approved by the mortgage holder.

Very Important

Just from reviewing some of the lease clause, you can see leases are complex contracts. As a landlord your lease is extremely important to protect you and to create a fair understanding with your tenants. Do not use "standard leases" forms from stationary stores or from the internet. Hire an attorney to create your lease and protect you.

Value = $80,000

∠TV = 80%

Term = 10 years

rate = 5 %

Amount = $64,000

Down Payment = $16,000.00

PI = $679.00

Part 7
Selling Your Property

Potential income = 13,800
Rental

Plus   Other income = $0

Less   Vacancy/credit loss = 800   94% Vacancy!

Gross operating income = $13,000

Operating expenses
Utilities = 2,100
water =
Sewer =

Legal/Accounting =

Annual debt service = 8,148

NOIE Net operating income = 2,752

COC (cash on cash) = 17.2%

10 year

holding
period

End of y/0 Cap rate =

Sales Price =

Chapter 18: Selling your Property and Capital Gains Taxes

Ready to Sell?

We started out this book discussing timing to buy; now is it the right time to sell? You have been taught to do a financial analysis and determine NOI and market value. Find out the CAP Rates from the local commercial banks when you are ready to sell and determine the value of your property. That is a good start.

But now you need some professional help because, if you are not in the real estate business, you do not the current market conditions, what other similar properties have sold for or how long those sale took. You may want to hire a professional Appraiser or a Commercial Real Estate Broker to help you with the evaluation. Plus a Broker has all the tools and resources to market your property.

"Holding Paper"

If you now have little or no debt, you may wish to sell and "hold paper"; offering to provide the mortgage loan. This gives you several advantages. You may require a smaller down payment that the banks do perhaps 20% down, in so doing you increase the pool of potential buyers. If the buyer defaults on the loan, you get the property back to sell again. The capital gains taxes on the sale are spread out over the term of the loan; only paying the tax on the principal collected each year.

Sales Options

Sometimes a buyer requires a change of use or zoning and this process can take a long time. They may be asking you to take your property off the market for 6 months or longer so they can get the zoning approval. Do you want to do this? What are the odds on their getting the zoning change?

Here is a suggestion, enter into a **Sales Option.** You agree to sell them the property for a specific amount of money at, for example, the end of one year. They agree to pay you a certain amount of money for taking your property off the market for that time. You are paid now and you keep the money whether or not they get their approvals. Be sure when you calculate the amount of your compensation to include any expenses you may have during that time; what would you have to pay in taxes, insurance, etc. during that period.

Selling your real estate: your home, commercial or investment property is a taxable event. You will most likely have to pay Capital Gains Taxes, <u>before putting your property on the market consult with your accountant or tax advisor.</u>

Capital Gains Taxes

Capital Gain is the profit realized from the sale of any capital investment including real estate.

Short Term Capital Gains are:

- Assets held for less than one year
- Taxed at the marginal rate of the taxpayers income

Long Term Capital Gains are:

- Assets held for 12 months and sold after May 5, 2003

This includes:

- Principal Residence
- Commercial Properties
- Investment Properties

Capital Losses:

- Capital losses occur when an investment or other types of property are sold at a loss
- Capital gains can be reduced by capital losses
- Net capital losses may be deducted from taxable income up to $3,000 per year and the unused loss may be "carried over" to future years until used up.

Tax Changes in 2018 that affect the sale of property

The Capital Gains Tax rates remained the same 15% or 20% tax on appreciation of value but the thresholds have changed, and will change each year based on inflation. The Medicare Surcharge would also be due at the point of sale, as would the Depreciation Recapture tax of 25%.

Single Taxpayer	Married Taxpayer	Capital Gains Tax Rate	Subject to NIT Net Investment Tax
Up to $38,600	Up to $77,200	0	0
$38,601 - $200,000	$77,201- $250,000	15%	0
$200,001 - $425,400	$250,001 - $479,000	15%	3.8%
$425,401 and up	$479,001	20%	3.8%

Already getting taxed on $432,720.00
So $432,720.00 -

Sale of your Primary/Principal Residence

The profit made from selling your personal residence is subject to a Capital Gains Tax based upon your taxable income level. However, the IRS provides a "Residential Exclusion":

- Homeowners may exclude the first $250,000 in gain ($500,000 if married and filing jointly) on the sale of one home every two years
- To be eligible home seller must have owned and resided in the home for two of the last five years before the sale

Terms:
- "Basis" – usually the cost of a property.
- "Adjusted Basis" – is the original cost or basis plus certain additions and minus certain deductions. An increase in Basis will reduce the taxable gain.

Buyers may add these costs to the Basis:
- Title Abstracts
- Title Insurance
- Attorneys Fees

Sellers may add these costs to the basis:
- Transfer Taxes
- Attorneys Fees
- Real Estate Commissions
- Residential - repairs made to the house within 90 days of the sale

In many areas property values are at a level where the Residential Exclusion is sufficient to avoid a taxable gain.

However in other areas property values are high and a sale may be subject to a Capital Gains Tax. If you are in this category be sure to discuss the sale with your accountant or tax advisor.

Sale of Personal Residential - Example of Capital Gains Tax

The value of Capital Improvements made to your home may be added to the purchase price. The resulting "adjusted basis" and the cost of the sale (i.e. legal fees, real estate commissions, and transfer taxes) are subtracted from the sales price to determine the net profits. Eligible exclusions may then reduce the taxable net profits further.

Example 1 - Married Couple selling their home*

Purchase price (20 years ago)	$125,000
Improvements (added a room)	+ 30,000
Adjusted Basis	$155,000
Sale Price	$895,000
Less Adjusted Basis	-155,000
Less Cost of Sale	-57,280
Net Profits	$682,720
Capital Gain Exclusion	-500,000*
Capital Gain	$182,720
Capital Gains Tax (15%)	**$27,408**

*married, filing jointly, have lived in the hone two out of the last five years.

Example 2 – Single Person selling their home, same example

Purchase price (20 years ago)	$125,000
Improvements	+ 30,000
Adjusted Basis	$155,000
Sale Price	$895,000
Less Adjusted Basis	-155,000
Less Cost of Sale	-57,280
Net Profits	$682,720
Capital Gain Exclusion	-250,000
Capital Gain	$432,720
Capital Gains Tax (20%)	**$86,544**
Medicare Surtax ($232,720 X .038)	**$8,843**

Handwritten notes in right margin:
Purchase Price 128,000
improvements 30,000
Adjusted bases 155,000
Sales Price

The single person only gets $250,000 exclusion; generating a capital gain that now exceeds the $425,000 threshold for single taxpayers. The Capital Gain will be taxed at 20%. Also since his/her income is over $200,000 it triggers the Medicare Surcharge Tax on the income over $200,000, for a total tax liability of $95,387.

Be aware, many States also have a Capital Gains Tax.

Sale of Commercial and investment Property

When it comes to commercial or investment property almost everyone has heard someone say, **"I can't sell my property; the Capital Gains Taxes will kill me!"** What does that really mean; how bad are these taxes?

We previously examined the Capital Gains Taxes on the sale of your Personal Residence; now we will examine the effect on commercial and investment properties.

Key Concept

With Commercial and Investment properties there are two Capital Gains Taxes. The first applies to the net gain or profit from the sale and is considered a tax on "appreciation" of value. The second is a tax on "depreciation recapture". Depreciation is not permitted to be taken on your personal residence; hence there is no Depreciation Recapture Tax on the sale of your home.

Terms:

- "Basis" – usually the cost of a property
- "Adjusted Basis" – is the original cost or basis plus capital improvements minus certain deductions such as depreciation and casualty losses
- Sale income may include any liabilities assumed by the buyer (i.e. taxes or mortgage)

Net Profits Defined:

Contract Sale Price

Less Adjusted Basis

Less Cost of Sale

Equals Net Profits

Capital Gains Taxes:

- The appreciation in value of Commercial and Investment properties, subject to adjustments, is taxed based upon the taxpayers tax bracket from 0% to 20% (as we noted in the chart on page 173).
- There is a second tax known as "Depreciation Recapture" at a 25% tax rate. This tax applies to commercial and investment properties only, not the sale of your personal residence.
- Many States have additional Capital Gains Taxes.

Depreciation Recapture Tax:

In a previous chapter we examined the concept and benefits of depreciation. However when commercial or investment property is sold there is a second Capital Gains Tax called the Depreciation Recapture Tax. Depreciation taken on the building and any capital improvement to the building during the ownership period is subject to a recapture tax of 25%.

Commercial Building Capital Gains Tax Example

A commercial Office building was purchased 20 years ago for $125,000. It was improved in stages totaling $130,000. Today it is being sold for $895,000.

What are the Capital Gains Taxes?

Step 1 Determine Adjusted Basis:

To do so first requires a calculation of depreciation taken to date.

Calculate Depreciation on the Building

Purchase price (20 yrs ago)	$125,000
Less Land Value	-$25,000
Building Value	$100,000

Depreciation taken to date on the building.

$100,000 ÷ 39 years = $2,564 per year

$2,564 X 20 years = $51,282

Depreciation (39 year schedule) $51,282

Depreciation must also be taken on Capital Improvements. Improvements may have been made at various times creating multiple depreciation schedules.

As discussed in Chapter 13 "Depreciation and Cost Recovery" Leasehold Improvements a/k/a Tenant Improvements (TI) are now defined as Qualified Improvements to the interior of nonresidential properties and are depreciated over 15 years. Excluded are building expansions, elevators, escalators or structural repairs. Currently these items may be eligible for bonus depreciation or Section 179 deductions.

For this example we will assume the depreciation on capital improvements taken to date of sale was $35,000.

Calculation the total depreciation taken:

Improvements Basis	$130,000
Depreciation taken on improvements to date	$35,000

Total Depreciation taken:

Building	$51,282
Improvements	+$35,000
Total	$86,282

The "Adjusted Basis" is determined by adjusting the "Basis" which is the Purchase Price, by adding the value of Capital Improvements made, and subtracting the amount of Depreciation taken during the period of ownership.

Calculating Adjusted Basis:

Purchase price (20 yrs ago)	$125,000
+ Improvements	+130,000
- Depreciation	-86,282
Adjusted Basis	$168,718

Step 2 Calculate the Capital gain

The Capital Gain is determined by subtracting from the sales price the "adjusted basis" and costs of the sale, what remains are the net profits; this is the Capital Gain subject to taxation.

Calculating Capital Gain:

Sale Price	$895,000
Less Adjusted Basis	-168,718
Less Cost of Sale	-57,280
Net Profits (Capital Gain)	$669,002

Step 3 Calculate the Capital Gains Taxes

Calculating Capital gains Taxes:

For tax calculation purposes the Net Profits are separated as to the gain from depreciation and the gain from "appreciation".

Total Capital Gains	$669,002
Gain from Depreciation	$86,282
Gain from Appreciation	$582,720

Depreciation Recapture Tax (25%) $86,282 X .25 = $21,570

The taxpayer is in the 20% Capital Gains Tax Bracket:

Tax on Appreciation (20%) $582,720 X .20 = $116,544

The taxpayer may also be subject to the Medicare Surcharge Tax based on their income:

Medicare Surcharge Tax (3.8%)

If Single: $669,002 - $200,000 = $469,002 X .038 = $17,822

If Married, filing jointly $669,002 - $250,000 = $419,002 X .038 = $15,922

Consequently the Total Capital Gains Taxes and Medicare Surcharge on a sale of $895,000 can range between $154,036 and $155,936 (plus State tax).

These are examples. Be sure to speak to your account or tax advisor to review your specific situation.

That's the problem! However there is a way to defer the Capital Gains Taxes by doing a "1031 Tax Deferred Exchange", which we will explore in the next chapter.

Remember this is the Federal Capital Gains Tax; many States also have an additional Capital Gains Tax.

Income Tax
Corporate Tax
Capital Gain Tax
Goods, Service
& Profits
(Sales tax)

(Small Business tax)

Chapter 19: 1031 Tax Deferred Exchanges

1031 Tax Deferred Exchanges

A 1031 Exchange allows the seller of real estate to defer the capital gains taxes on that sale (the relinquished property) by buying another real estate property (the replacement property).

There are many rules and requirements for exchanges. It is required by the IRS that the taxpayer have an independent third party conduct the exchange generally referred to as the Qualified Intermediary.

One of the rules prohibits the taxpayer or any attorney, accountant or real estate agent they have worked with within the last two years from serving as the Qualified Intermediary (QI).

Exchanges are considered to be "federal" in nature as properties in one state can be exchanged for properties in another. Consequently there are no licensing requirements for Qualified Intermediaries. (But, check with your State, requirements may change.) Unfortunately, this has led to some criminal activity on the part of some unscrupulous QI's.

Many Title Companies and some banks have gone into the 1031 Exchange business and offer this service. Independent practitioners should be questioned about their fiduciary policies; are they bonded, insurance guarantees, how is your money protected?

The way an exchange generally works is: the taxpayer will relinquished property title (of the property being sold) to the Intermediary, who will actually sell the property and hold the sale proceeds. Then the QI will act as the buyer of the replacement property being purchased. The QI prepares all the required documentation, provides complete accounting to the taxpayer and concludes by transferring the title of the newly acquired property to the taxpayer.

Qualified Properties

Prior to January 1, 2018 many types of properties were eligible for 1031 Exchanges; under the new tax laws 1031 Exchanges are restricted only to real property.

Replacement property acquired in an Exchange must be like kind to the property being relinquished. Like kind means "similar in nature or character, notwithstanding differences in grade or quality."   Different types of investment real property may be "exchanged", office buildings for retail centers, retail for industrial, industrial for multi-family or any combination thereof.

Both the relinquished and the replacement properties must be held by the Exchanger for investment purposes or for "productive use in their trade or business".

Your Personal Residence and Personal Property are not eligible for exchange.

General Rules

Identify the replacement property within 45 days after transfer of the relinquished property.

Receive title to the replacement property within 180 days after the transfer of the relinquished property.

All proceeds of the sale of the relinquished property must be held by a third party, a "Qualified Intermediary".

All cash proceeds must be invested to fully defer taxable gain.

Three Acquisition Rules

The Three-Investment Property Rule states that the exchanger must identify up to, but no more than three potential investment properties during the acquisition period. OR

(no more)

The Two Hundred Percent Rule - This rule dictates that, in the event that three or more like kind investment properties are selected as replacement investment properties, the aggregate market value of said investment properties may not exceed 200% of the market value of relinquished investment property. OR

The Ninety-five Percent Exception. If Exchanger identifies more than three properties which are worth more than 200% of the value of all relinquished properties then Exchanger must acquire 95% of the value of all properties identified.

200%

Full and Partial Exchanges

When all the proceeds of the sale are used to purchase a replacement property and the value, equity and debt are all "equal to or greater than" a full deferral of the Capital Gains Tax is possible. If all these rules are not complied with a partial deferral of the taxes may be possible.

"Boot" – A term used to describe other non-qualified property received in an exchange, that is not like kind to the property acquired. (cash, stock, personal property)

The "boot" proceeds in the exchange are considered a gain and are taxable.

For a full deferral of capital gains taxes the value, equity and debt must be "equal to or greater than".

Example 1

Full Deferral of Capital Gains Tax	Relinquished Sold Property	Replacement Purchased
Value	$450,000	$600,000
Equity	$200,000	$200,000
Debt	$250,000	$400,000

✓ Full deferal of tax

In this case each category is "equal to or greater than".

Example 2

Partial Deferral of Capital Gains Tax	Relinquished Sold Property	Replacement Purchased
Value	$450,000	$600,000
Equity	$200,000	**$150,000**
Debt	$250,000	$450,000

Purchase cost
+
100 % Rehab
+
Closing cost
70,000

$100,000
− 78,368
_____

In this case the Equity is reduced (not equal to or greater than)
Cash Boot of $50,000; subject to Capital Gains Tax

742.00
X 12
_____
8,904 + 64,464 + 5,000

185

Example 3

Partial Deferral of Capital Gains Tax	Relinquished Sold Property	Replacement Purchased
Value	$450,000	**$350,000**
Equity	$200,000	$200,000
Debt	$250,000	**$150,000**

In this case the replacement property value and mortgage are reduced creating Mortgage Boot of $100,000; subject to Capital Gains Tax

The IRS requires that the taxpayer be "arms distant" from the 1031 Exchange. Be sure to consult with a Qualified Intermediary.

History of Exchanges

The Revenue Act of 1918 was the first income tax code in the United States, it did not address exchanges. In 1921 the code was modified and included the first definitions of tax deferred exchanges. Further revisions occurred in subsequent years, in 1935 the foundations of the current statutes were established, including defining the Qualified Intermediary (Accommodator). At that time the statute was known as section 112 of the tax code. In 1954, the statute was changed to section 1031.

Prior to 1979 exchanges were accomplished in a one day long closing; the relinquished property being sold followed by the replacement property being purchased.

T.J. Starker and his son sold timberland to Crown Zellerback, Inc. in exchange for a contract to acquire certain properties within 5 years. The IRS disallowed this "delayed" exchange. In 1979 the Starker Family sued the IRS and won the case setting precedent for today's non-simultaneous, delayed tax deferred exchanges. In 1984 Congress adopted the 45 calendar day identification Period and the 180 calendar day Exchange Period; imposing a limit on the length of the exchange opportunity.

The Tax Reform Act of 1986 restricted tax benefits of owning real estate and really catapulted 1031 exchanges into the forefront. The act eliminated preferred capital gains treatment, taxing them as ordinary income; eliminated accelerated depreciation in favor of straight line over 27.5 years for residential property and 39 years for commercial property.

In 1990 the IRS issued comprehensive Tax-Deferred Exchange Regulations which for the most part are today's guidelines. Two additional advances have occurred since, in 2002 fractional or co-ownership of real estate known as Tenant-In-Common ownership was authorized to be used in an exchange. In 2004 Delaware Statutory Trusts were ruled as being real estate and therefore as a replacement property solution for 1031 exchanges.

Comparing Tenants-in-Common and Delaware Statutory Trusts

Tenants-in-Common and Delaware Statutory Trusts are similar in that either may be used in a 1031 Exchange and both give the investor an opportunity for participation in a larger project; but they are also quite different.

One of the most difficult parts of doing a 1031 Tax Deferred Exchange is finding the right replacement property to purchase within the required 45 day identification period, and successfully closing the purchase within 180 days. Additional exchange opportunities of large investment grade buildings are offered by many firms as Tenant-in-Common (TIC) or Delaware Statutory Trusts (DST).

With Tenants-in-Common you own a pro-rate share of a building. In this structure each investor forms a single member limited liability company and the lender is financing individually with each investor. Each investor reaps their proportionate share of cash flows and eventual sale proceeds. But this structure can become convoluted as investors in the TIC must vote unanimously on all major investment decisions. It may become difficult to get all the co-investors to agree on an important decision.

One of the TIC rules is there can be no more than 35 co-investors. Practically speaking this limits the amount of funds available; say each investor contributes $100,000 and loans are secured for 50% of the value; the available funds to purchase are $7,000,000.

The Delaware Statutory Trust is governed by the Security and Exchange Commission (SEC) regulation D of the 1933 Securities Act and later defined in 2010 by the Dodd-Frank Act. This requires each investor to be an "Accredited Investor". These are individuals whose net worth is in excess of $1 million and/or earned annual income of $200,000 for two or more years, with expectation that this income level will continue. Typical DST's will have a 100 (sometimes more) investors, allowing then to raise significantly more capital and buy much larger buildings than with a TIC.

With the DST there are property sponsors who serve as Trustees of the Trust; they purchase the property and structure it as a securities DST, with written detailed offering documents. Mortgage banking and property management are pre-arranged by the property sponsor. The investor owns an individual "Beneficial Interest" in the DST; there is no need to form individual LLC's. The Trust owns 100% of the real estate so unlike the TIC there is only one loan and one borrower.

The property sponsor administers the Trust and operations of the property. Management is less complicated as individual co-investors or beneficiaries in a Delaware Statutory Trust are not permitted to vote. There are numerous other rules and regulations regarding the DST operations.

Both TIC's and DST's can be set up as income producing properties; other offerings may have the strategy of directing all the income to pay down the loan, thereby increasing each taxpayer's equity over the course of the holding period. Upon disposition of the asset the taxpayer can potentially use another 1031 exchange, and do this all over again!

This is just a brief outline of these types of investments; be sure you or your client discusses these opportunities with your accountant and an expert in either Tenants-in-Common or Delaware Statutory Trusts.

Part 8
More to Know

Chapter 20: Real Estate Brokers

Your market expert is your local **Commercial** Real Estate Broker. You need to work with someone experienced and trained in commercial real estate. They can provide you with current market values and trends, they know the available inventory, where to find buyers or tenants and assist in the negotiations of a sale or lease.

As an owner of investment property one of your biggest concerns is keeping your property fully rented. Vacancy costs you money. You want financially solid tenants who will sign as long a lease as possible.

Brokers work very hard to be the experts in their market and they **only get paid after doing all the work,** when the sale closes or when the lease is signed.

Exclusive Listing Agreements

Brokers will ask you to sign an Exclusive Brokerage Agreement with them. Interview a number of brokerage firms and select the one you are most comfortable with based upon their experience in handling your type of property. It is recommended you sign an Exclusive Listing Agreement with this broker. It is also recommended that you have your attorney review it first. **An Exclusive Agreement gives the broker the responsibility and fiduciary duty to do what is in your best interest; to negotiate on your behalf, to get you the best deal possible.**

It is the job of the Exclusive Broker to advise the availability of the sale or leasing of your property with all the other brokers in the market. The Exclusive Broker should be willing to Co-Broke (and share the commission fee) with other brokers who may have a buyer or tenant for your property.

There are many Commercial Listing Services available to help promote your property. Some have public access others only have access to brokers who subscribe to those services. **In order for a broker to post properties on these Commercial Listing services the broker must have a signed Exclusive Listing Agreement.** In order to get the maximum exposure for your property it is essential you select one brokerage firm to represent you exclusively and sign an Exclusive Listing Agreement with them.

Exclusive Buyer Brokerage or Tenant Representation Agreements

Generally, in commercial real estate the seller or the landlord is expected to pay the commission or fees to the broker(s). It is possible for a buyer or tenant to enter into an Exclusive Listing Agreement with a broker. **An Exclusive Agreement gives the broker the responsibility and fiduciary duty to do what is in your best interest; to negotiate in your behalf, to get you the best deal possible.**

This type of agreement will require the buyer or tenant to commit to paying the broker commission or fee. However, most agreements have language that states: "if the broker collects all or part of their fee from the owner or landlord, that money will be credited against what the buyer or tenant has agreed to pay".

These agreements give the broker the freedom to approach owners, landlords or other brokers with suitable listings, knowing if they are offered no commission or a reduced commission they will still get paid by you. Your best opportunity or location may be in a brokerage (fee) hampered building or a property not on the market. With an Exclusive Buyer Broker or Exclusive Tenant Representation Agreement your Broker can now bring that opportunity to you.

Commissions or Professional Service Fees

All Commissions or Professional Service Fees are negotiable but remember an old adage: "you get what you pay for". A Broker who discounts their fee below typical market rates may not have the skills, resources or experience to negotiate the best deal for you.

Broker fees are generally based upon all the monies received by the seller or landlord. A single rate of commission may be negotiated and be applied to the selling price or the aggregate rental value in the case of a lease.

The following examples are for illustrative purposes; all commission fees are negotiable.

Sales Commission - For example: It may be agreed in a sale that the seller will pay 7% of the sales price of the property as a commission fee to the Broker upon closing.

Lease Fees may be calculated using various formulas.

Aggregate Commission Fee – Example: A five year lease, the landlord is collecting $50,000 a year in rent (we will keep the example simple and not include annual rent increases).

The aggregate rental value over the five years is $250,000 ($50,000 X 5 years). The agreed fee is 5%. In this case the broker's commission would be $12,500. ($250,000 X 5% = $12,500).

In many areas lease commissions are calculated on sliding scales. This is known as the **Split-Rate Commission Formula.** This may be applied in different ways in different areas. Here are two examples:

The fee will be based upon 7% of the gross annual rent for the first three years and upon 3% of the gross annual rent for each year thereafter.

Or on a five year lease: The commission is based upon 6% of the first years rent, 4% of the second and third years rent and 3% of the fourth and fifth years rent.

This is the method of calculation and it would be figured including the rent escalations. The total amount of the commission or fee is due and payable upon lease signing.

If there are options, extensions or expansions of the lease and these are exercised giving the landlord additional rent from this tenant, **the broker would be entitled to an additional fee at that time.**

The fee may also be based upon monthly rental values; for example in a short three year lease the fee may be the equivalent of three month rent.

A Fixed Fee may also be charged if the broker is hired to rent multiple spaces in a building. There are ten units to be rented, the Fixed Fee for each signed lease will be $25,000.

Override Commissions – Used in difficult or declining markets where there is a lot of vacancy or competition for tenants. The Exclusive Broker will be coordinating the leasing with all the other brokers in the market. To entice them to focus on this property it may be necessary to offer them a full commission, the listing broker still needs to get paid so the fee in this case would by 1 ½ times the agreed commission.

What do Brokers do?

Commission fees may seem like a lot of money, but remember Brokers do all of the work upfront and only get paid if your property is sold or a lease is signed.

Brokers are constantly monitoring local marketing conditions and sales activity to be able to guide you in pricing your property correctly. Once your property is listed they do extensive marketing by, creating flyers, brochures, and/or videos; which must then be distributed. Sending mailings, emails, and texts to their potential customers, the surrounding businesses in the area, and other commercial Brokerages firms in the area offering to co-broke with them. Internet marketing today is essential, which requires them to subscribe to various Commercial Listing services.

As interest builds for your property, they need to qualify potential buyers and tenants, do they have the money? Showings are next, which lead to offers to buy or lease your property. The negotiation phase follows where they will work for you to get you the best deal possible. In a sale, the contract is only the beginning; brokers will be there for the property inspection, environmental testing , and the bank appraiser, doing what they can to assist in moving the deal forward. With lease they will work through all the issues to get an acceptable Letter of Intent; which should be sent to your attorney to draft a lease. When the lease is drawn the Broker will review to be sure all agreed issues are in it, nothing more or less. (This extra set of "eyes" can be very helpful to be sure nothing is missed or was misunderstood.)

Your Broker may help you find and buy another building, especially if you are doing a 1031 exchange or be ready to find you another tenant when you have another vacancy in your building.

Assumption Agreements

We previously mentioned that if there are options, extensions or expansions of the lease and these are exercised giving the landlord additional rent from the tenant, the broker would be entitled to an additional fee at that time.

But what happens if the building is sold before the option becomes due or an expansion is requested? **The Broker will be concerned about getting paid their fee**. Is the new owner responsible to pay the Brokers commission? The answer is no, unless the listing agreement or lease addresses the issue.

The original listing agreement (contract) is between the original owner and the Broker, upon sale of the building (title passing or closing) that relationship ends. The Broker has no agreement (contract) with the new owner. The new owner has no obligation to pay a commission to the Broker. This may also apply to an Exchange or Assignment of a Lease.

Brokers will make sure their Listing agreements contain a clause to address this contingency. Typically the clause directs the building owner, if they decide to sell the property, to have the buyer sign an **Assumption Agreement** (in recordable form). In so doing the new owner accepts the liability for future Brokers commissions that may become due if a tenant exercises their option to extend the lease.

In a large building many tenants may have an option to extend or renew their leases; different Brokers may be eligible for future commissions. **Sellers and Buyers need to be aware of these possibilities; the amount of money involved could be significant and require adjustments in closing the transaction.**

Paying Broker Commissions or Tenant Improvement Expenses

A Broker's Commission or Fee for a long term lease can be a lot of money, and they expect to be paid on lease signing. To get a great new tenant to sign a long term lease may require the owner paying a lot of money for Tenant Improvements. Where or how can the landlord get the necessary funding to pay these obligations?

It certainly may be possible to borrow money, get a bank loan, especially if you have a "Credit Worthy" or National Tenant. But another technique that may possibly be used is **Prepaid Rent.** Asking the tenant to pay four, five or six months rent at lease signing to cover your expenses. Many of the stronger tenants have the financial capabilities of doing so.

This needs to be structured carefully so it does not affect your cash flow. If this was your first six months rent, you may not be able to pay your expenses during that period. What is typically done is the Prepaid Rent would represent the rent payments for the following months: 1st month, 13th month, 25th month, 37th month, 49th month and 61st month. In this way you are still collecting 11 months rent each year. You need to be sure that 11 payments during these years will be sufficient to pay your expenses and any loan obligations for the entire year. If so, this technique will provide the solution to this challenge.

Develop Relationships with Brokers

Hire a professional real estate broker to assist you with your real estate transactions. Their market knowledge and marketing skills will save you money in the long run.

Chapter 21: Getting Started

Your Financial Situation

What can you afford to invest in?

We have seen the latest real estate cycle; crash in 2007-2008 where commercial property values dropped 25%, 30%, or more depending on the market you are in. Financing became difficult; banks underwriting standards become more stringent. Commercial "bottomed out in 2013 and has been moving positively to today (2018). In many places values have been restored to pre-2007 levels or higher.

Current financing of commercial property requires a minimum of 30%, to 40% down payment. But funding is available. The exception being Small Business Administration (SBA) financing. If you will occupy the building yourself (at least 51% of the building) you may qualify for up to 90% financing.

Do not guess, do not assume. If you are contemplating investing in real estate find out your financial facts. Talk to your accountant, attorney, financial advisor and several banks. Know what you will need as a realistic down payment; know how much money you can borrow for your investment and what will be your cost to repay your loan. Does the potential return on your investment make financial sense?

Getting Advice

You also need to know the market conditions and opportunities, consult with a real estate professional that specializes in commercial and investment brokerage. You need a broker (agent) who can find you a building to buy, fill it with tenants and sell the property later. Look to develop a long term relationship, enter into appropriate exclusive agreements and pay the required fee for services. This is not the time for discounted talent or fees.

Remember brokers do this everyday and they have resources you do not. Their relationships with other buyers and sellers allow them to find properties and opportunities that may not yet be on the market.

Finding Properties

Today's consumer has access to many of the Commercial Listing Service web sites directly. Some sites are free but most are by subscription. Viewing buildings that are your "competition" can give you an idea of values or pricing in your area.

Some of the more common web sites are:

Your local Multiple Listing Service (MLS); most have a commercial section.

www.commercialsearch.com - This is the National Association of Realtors Commercial web site

www.loopnet.com – Considered being the largest commercial data base web site, it allows you to register for free with limited access. You must subscribe for access.

www.CoStar.com – This site is restricted to the trade and is very comprehensive. They do offer listing to the public view through their www.Showcase.com site for free.

www.CIMLS.com; and www.commrex.com are a few others. Different sites are available in different locations.

Search the internet under Commercial Real Estate and other related topics for more sites, and the web site addresses of National and local Commercial Real Estate Brokerage Firms.

Conclusion

Real Estate investing can be vey lucrative but it does have its risks. Understanding the numbers, the terms used in the trade, financial analysis, mortgage underwriting, the formulas, determining values and leasing issues and clauses are the keys to help you make the right decisions and take advantage of today's opportunities. I hope you have found this book informative and helpful.

This is a great time to invest in real estate!

Made in the
USA
Lexington, KY